C000125767

P.P. Bliss

SONG WRITER

WILLIAM GUEST

~ *INTRODUCTION BY D. L. MOODY* ~

AMBASSADOR

BELFAST ◆ **GREENVILLE**
NORTHERN IRELAND   SOUTH CAROLINA

First published 1877
This edition 1997

All rights reserved

ISBN 1 84030 008   6

AMBASSADOR PRODUCTIONS LTD,
Providence House
16 Hillview Avenue,
Belfast, BT5 6JR
Northern Ireland

Emerald House,
1 Chick Springs Road, Suite 206
Greenville,
South Carolina 29609
United States of America

Introduction by D. L. Moody.

 HAVE pleasure in giving a word of introduction to the Memoirs of my dear friend and brother, P. P. Bliss.

I regret the little time at my disposal prevents my writing more fully concerning THE MAN and HIS WORK. I could probably add nothing to the facts of his life that are here compiled, but I should like to tell something of how I loved and admired him.

I believe he was raised up of God to write hymns for the Church of Christ in this age, as Charles Wesley was for the Church in his day. His Songs have gone around the world, and have led and will continue to lead hundreds of souls to Christ.

In my estimate, he was the most highly honoured of God of any man of his time, as a writer and singer of Gospel Songs; and, with all his gifts, he was the most humble man I ever knew. I loved him as a brother, and shall cherish his memory, giving praise to God for the grace manifested in him, while life lasts.

D L Moody

BOSTON, *February,* 1877.

P. P. Bliss:
His Life and Life-Work.

— ◆ —

Prefatory.

THE pleasant duty of presenting to English readers a brief but remarkable history of a rare Christian and singularly influential man has been committed to me by Messrs. Morgan and Scott. It must, however, be understood that the facts, dates, and incidents of the narrative have been derived from the records and contributions supplied by Major D. W. Whittle, who was a personal friend of Mr. Bliss, and his colleague in evangelistic labours.

In preparing the English Edition, it has seemed desirable to re-write most of the Life ; to entirely re-arrange the materials ; and to supply links that were missing in the original narrative, by interweaving passages from the letters and tributes of regard which were placed elsewhere in the American edition. For opinions interspersed I must be held responsible.

I venture to supplement Mr. Moody's Introduction by one or two statements that may better enable English readers to understand the special work of Mr. Bliss.

It is scarcely five months since he and his gifted wife
passed to their blessedness in circumstances inexpressibly
affecting. The first thirty years of his life were years of
preparation ; the last seven have unquestionably left their
mark on the development of the Christian Church in the
two hemispheres.

Clearly a religious movement, with peculiar and extensive
results, has during the last seven years powerfully affected
vast multitudes of persons in America and the British Isles.
At a time when the masses of the population were drifting
more and more from churches, and from Christianity, they
have been largely brought under the influence of the primary
truths of the Gospel by a new and informal method of
evangelistic labour. It would exceedingly astonish those
whose attention has not been turned to the subject, to learn
the change that has passed over certain classes of society
since the close of the year 1869. The Christian Church
has also shared in the advantage. The social services of
religion have become brighter ; and music, which has been
called " the speech of the angels," has spoken " straight to
men's hearts, spirits, and to the very core and root of their
souls."

It is not too much to say that no one man has more contributed to these results, or done more to popularize this
religious movement than PHILIP PAUL BLISS. He was too
modest to comprehend his own work. He aimed at nothing
lofty ; but he wrote songs and hymns, and, as a composer,
invested them with a musical clothing, and they have
melted, soothed, and animated vast numbers of persons, and
have become "familiar as household words."

Nor can it be said that the effect will be transient.
Hymns and music are a powerful element of Christian
advancement, and some of Mr. Bliss's hymns will be long
used by devout persons. Those that appear in the " Later

Songs and Solos " are richer in their harmonies and accordant notes than the earlier ones ; these are only now beginning to be known in England. It may be objected with candour that Mr. Bliss did not study a scientific class of music, and did not possess high poetical genius. The fact, however, remains, that wherever his hymns and music are sung with appropriate feeling, which must be demanded for all music, they have touched men's hearts, and have given new conceptions of the Gospel, as the message of heaven's mercy to our poor, tempted, and sinful race. It is no doubt true that the introduction of singing into evangelistic services, not as an act of direct worship, but as conveying great truths to human hearts, was a new thing : but the readers of Charles Kingsley's Life will recall his statement (vol. ii., p. 93)—" All revivals of religion which I ever read of, which produced a permanent effect, owed their strength to the introduction of some new element."

But it is not merely as a man who had the instincts of a musical composer that Mr. Bliss must be regarded. There was a moral grandeur about his noble meekness, sweetness of temper, and aspiring enthusiasm to fill life with brightness. His dignity, sympathy, affectionateness, courtesy, and joyousness invest his character with great loveliness. He was a holy man, but his holiness was genial and cheery. His perfect disinterestedness became a spell of ascendancy. His manliness, unassuming temper, and catholic spirit drew to him the love of Christians of all denominations, and this Memoir will show how cordial to him was the attachment of ministers of all evangelical churches. His wealth of rich emotion and high endowments made him a fitting instrument to win favour for that aggressive religious movement which is destined, if treated with confidence, to bless men increasingly.

I trust, therefore, that through God's grace the history

of PHILIP PAUL BLISS will soften any prejudice that
may exist with respect to a movement with which his
name is identified, will invest with a new interest those
hymns of his which are sung everywhere in homes and
religious meetings, and will impart to us all an impulse to
imitate that goodness which is only perfect in Him whom
he sought to exalt by word and song.

WILLIAM GUEST.

MILTON-ON-THAMES, KENT,
    May, 1877.

Chapter I.

Mr. Bliss's Ancestry—His Father, John Bliss—His Early Days—Love for Music—First Sight of a Piano—Connection with the Church—Influence of a Pious Father's Example—First Musical Instruction—W. B. Bradbury ; and Mr. Bliss's Tribute to his Memory.

N the forest and mountain region of Northern Pennsylvania PHILIP PAUL BLISS was born, on July 9th, 1838. His mother bore the name of grand Puritan celebrity—that of Doolittle. She possessed the strength, patience, and wisdom of the ancestral line, and was pre-eminently a woman of prayer. His father, John Bliss, descended from an ancestor who emigrated from Wales in the days of religious persecution, and who married in 1670 Damaris Arnold, the daughter of "Governor Arnold," of Connecticut.

Of John Bliss, the father, his son Philip penned the filial eulogy, "He was the best man I ever knew." Nor was this a partial testimony. He was long spoken of among his neighbours as a man of "fine simplicity, lovely tenderness, and devoted piety." Descended from the Puritans, he thought that something of austerity was consistent with his profession as a man who feared God; but his nature or his judgment got the better of his traditional convictions, and his son wrote respecting him :—

"He lived in continual communion with his Saviour, always happy, always trusting, always singing. My mother used sometimes to say to him, laughingly, that all his hymns commenced with the word 'Come;' and I can remember many of them that he used to sing. There were 'Come, ye sinners, poor and needy,' 'Come on, my partners in distress,' 'Come, ye that love the Lord.' He was always a poor man, but early in the morning, and after the toil of the day, in the evening, sitting in the porch of his humble home, his voice would be heard in song; and I can almost hear him now, singing upon the other side, 'Come to that happy land, come, come away.' He was a diligent reader of the Bible, and had the most implicit faith in its teachings, and a deep reverence for its commands. My first recollection of him is his daily family prayer. Devout, tender, and childlike, repeating over and over again, year after year, about the same words, until we all knew them by heart, his prayers were very real, very holy to me in my childhood. It was very hard for him ever to punish us; and when he did, he suffered more than we did. He would talk to us with great solicitude, and when we would say we were sorry, and would do better, he would be full of joy, and would say, 'That is right! That is right!'"

He says further of that time, " Whatever of plain living, small home, poor advantages, backwoods society, I had in my childhood, I cherish this precious thought—my parents prayed for me even before I knew the meaning of prayer, and consecrated me to the Lord, and His service."

Although it is not true that all men who have been used of God in a marked manner have had their first training in the discipline of suffering, it is nevertheless certain that some of the most distinguished men have risen to usefulness out of the hard school of poverty and early sorrows. Sympathy is the best and the most fruitful quality of human nature. No man ever left an ineffaceable line on the track of life without it. It is " the bearing of a yoke in the youth" that gives oft-times that sense of dependence, and that pathos of character, which become the foundation of eminence. Weakness is the channel for the in-coming of Divine strength. The reduced circumstances of the parents of Philip Bliss in those wilder parts of Pennsylvania made the boy a child of nature. He lived among the mountains; wandered alone by the side of babbling streams; listened to the voices and felt awed before "God's silence" in the forests. Barefooted, and with "patched clothing," he went out from that "log home," and

> His "life, exempt from public haunt,
> Found tongues in trees, books in the running brooks,
> Sermons in stones, and good in everything."

From the beginning a love of song grew with his years. As Edwards of Banff, poor as he was, watched the habits of animals, so Philip Bliss listened for their music. His childish ear was caught by any note in nature. Too poor to buy even the cheapest instrument, he would draw forth notes from reeds; and at seven years of age would manufacture instruments in a most original fashion, and reproduce for himself the tones he heard. When a boy of ten summers, he heard a piano for the first time. He stood entranced. The power of combining harmonies was a revelation to him. Sometimes he told the story in a graphic manner, with the history of the rebuke he received. He was then a poorly clad, overgrown boy; and one day, going down the village, and passing by a house, he heard music, sweeter than anything he had ever listened to before. The door stood open, and he was irresistibly drawn toward the sweet sounds that came from within. Barefooted, he entered unobserved, and stood at the parlour-door, listening and wondering, as a young lady played upon the piano. As she ceased playing, he exclaimed, with an intense desire, "Oh, lady, play some more." She looked around surprised, and, with no appreciation of the tender heart that had been so touched by her music, ordered him away. Crushed in spirit, he went forth, but with the memory of harmonies that seemed to him like heaven.

But nature treated him not thus. She loves to display her treasures to those who love her, and Philip Bliss drew from "a recollected love" when he wrote :

> " There's not a flower that decks the field,
> Nor bud by way-side bower concealed,
> Whose life a perfume rich doth yield,
>   But blooms for me.
>
> There's not a star in yon deep blue,
> That shines with radiance calm and true,
> Nor mirrored in the morning dew,
>   But shines for me.
>
> There's not a joy the heart can move,
> No pleasure here, no bliss above,
> No earthly weal, no heavenly love,
>   But waits for me."

Think not, however, of this child of nature as a pensive boy. His nature overflowed with gleesomeness. The love of fun he never lost. His earnest wife would sometimes tell him afterwards that he had carried the love of fun into his manhood. Song and music ran as a thread of gladness through the boy's nature ; and, like David, of "a beautiful countenance and goodly to look to," he won love then, as he continued to do till heaven claimed him as its own.

Most boys go to work when schooling is over. He went to work to gratify his eager thirst for learning. At thirteen years of age we find the tall, well-favoured boy working on a farm at Marvin for nine dollars a month. Happily, society in America, and a wonderful school system,

enable a farmer's boy to combine work and learning.
Every leisure moment is used by Philip to obtain the teaching of the School House. Literature opens for him its
exciting stores. Ceaseless is his application, until the thought
dawns on him that he also may become a teacher ; and when
he is eighteen years of age the School Board of Hartsville,
Alleghany County, New York, selects him for this position.
But something better than literature was touching the
springs of his nature. He always said he never could remember the time "when he was not sorry for sin, and did
not love Christ." In his fourteenth year, however, he
avowed himself a disciple of the Lord Jesus. The occasion of this was a religious awakening among his school-
fellows. Revivals of religion in schools are often treated
more than doubtfully. The mistrust, notwithstanding some
facts which are held to justify it, is a mistake. Not a few
of the noblest Christian men have been moulded and determined as to character by these juvenile pointings of their
nature Christward. Some of the best men and women of
our day received their new birth in revivals of religion.
Nothing is of more vital importance to a child than habits
of prayer and dependence on the Saviour. Only let a boy
trust, as Philip Bliss did, in the gentle patience and benignity
of Jesus towards him, and the good Spirit will make that
trust an atmosphere of growth for all that is lovely and
noble in character. The avowment of a youth for Christ
is also most helpful to an ingenuous nature. The open
confession of the Lord is often, by God's goodness, made
a wall of security against the temptations of the world.
The revival of religion was therefore useful to the "country
boy," as he always called himself; and it was well for him
that he united with the communicants who received the
memorials of the Lord's death from the hands of the pastor
who had conducted it.

After this he writes home :—

" For myself, I feel as strong in the Lord as ever, and have nothing discouraging to say to any one, and I thank God I am what I am, and am determined that nothing shall separate me from the love of Christ. Pray for me. I wish I could be at home to enjoy the good of the Meetings with you ; but you must remember me. Give my love to all who take the trouble to inquire after my welfare. Write often and give me all the news. When you have made any maple sugar, just send me word, and I will start for home, I reckon."

Philip became soon after this a Sunday-school teacher, as he continued most of his life. He carried the love of song into the school, and once reasoned with those who had not at that time learnt to appreciate the revolution as to the influence of hymns, which he did so much to introduce.

" Think," said he, " how readily children catch the meaning of a hymn, and how lasting may be its influence. Remember how many have been led to the cleansing Fountain through the instrumentality of song, when argument and entreaty have failed. Cannot you, yourself, now remember songs that you heard in childhood? More than this, can you not recall the very voice and manner in which they were sung? While the sermons—ably written, well delivered, with their flights of oratory and tender appeal—where are they ? Their very texts forgotten ! Their flashing brilliancy lost in the dark sea of forgetfulness, at least, so far as you are concerned. Not so the song. Many of us can remember the tunes and hymns sung in church last Sunday. How many can repeat the text from which the sermon was published ? "

When nineteen years of age Philip Bliss received his first instruction in music. He writes home thus :—

"TOWANDA, SUSQUEHANNA COLLEGIATE INSTITUTE,
August 26, 1857.

"DEAR FRIENDS,—You will see by the date of this that
I am here. And I can tell you I am well, and well satisfied,
too, with my situation, being now comfortably located in
the Institution, and I commenced my collegiate course to-
day. I put right down to Towanda, Monday afternoon,
after I came back from home afoot ; stayed over night ;
came up here Tuesday morning and did chores all day ;
got my board, and was allowed one dollar to apply on
tuition ; since that time have earned fifty cents. There is
a chance of my getting all the jobs of work I want to do,
which will pay my way. Board, lodging, washing, lights, and
fuel, room-rent included, cost me just two dollars per week.
Have a nice spacious room on the fourth floor, facing
Front Street, where I have a full view of the whole city
and suburbs. A very pleasant place this is, and the people
are very hospitable, especially the steward and his wife,
which will be of great benefit if I can retain their good will
and friendship, which, of course, I shall strive to do. I am
a kind of chore-boy, but I am not ashamed of it. I saw
wood, bring water, sweep rooms at so much a-piece, and am
resolved to earn every penny I possibly can honourably.

"To-day we commenced ; just organized. I intended to
go to some other school than this, but I could not have
been better situated. Hear what Mr. Dayton, the steward,
says : 'Come along to school one, two, or three terms, and
if you cannot pay me now, pay me after you have earned it ;
for if you teach this winter, you can then pay me ; so come
along.' So I've come ; and oh, how I wish I could afford
to stay about four years ! I won't complain, but '*do the
very best I can*,' you may be sure. I have taken up
Grammar, Algebra, Physiology, and Latin, for my studies
during the coming term.

"Towanda is twenty miles east of Troy, a direct line of stages running between, and a trusty stage-driver (lucky for me).

"I must close and save some for next time. Expecting to hear from you soon, I remain as ever,

"Your affectionate brother,

"PHILIP P. BLISS."

The lady who was Mr. Bliss's first instructor in music sent, after his death, the following interesting communication concerning this period :—

"Away back in 1857 I first met Mr. Bliss when he entered the Collegiate Institute at Towanda, in which school I then had charge of the department of music. His complete attention and excellence in the singing class brought him especially to my attention and esteem, and my every remembrance of him at that time is laden with some grace or goodness of character. Always in the true place at the right time, noble, modest, and courteous. Of wealth of heart and soul he possessed a princely store. A pure, fresh, sweet life, consecrated thus early to the Lord, unostentatious but sincerely glad to be heard in supplication or praise, and oft-times in the midst of Professors and pupils I have heard him in such humble, reverent prayer that I knew he had learned of Him who alone giveth such understanding.

"After long years of separation, after he had gained new friends, new dignities, and new honours, as well as superior mental and spiritual attainments, he came back to find me, with the gratitude and simplicity of a child, thanking me for what I had done for him, and begging still to call me 'Teacher,' which name I find in the last letter he wrote to me. In his wonderful friendship and fidelity, I have found strength, peace, and comfort. Always in my greatest need his letters came; and if in my invalid days I was ready to weep or faint or mourn, as I remembered some word or hymn or benediction of his, I found courage and peace."

In the latter part of 1857 we find him attending a Musical Convention at Rome, Pennsylvania. With this village of about three hundred inhabitants his life was to be largely associated. His visit now was specially remarkable as turning his attention to harmony more fully, and bringing him into acquaintance with Mr. W. B. Bradbury, who has composed many popular pieces of sacred music for children, and who was a man of fine sympathies. The Convention turned the thoughts of Mr. Bliss to the subject of sacred hymns and music for childhood. Subsequently he heard of the death of Mr. Bradbury, and wrote the lines which recall himself to multitudes now :—

> " We love him, though his friendly hand
>   Has never clasped our own;
> His gentle voice and loving smile
>   We never yet have known.
> We love the sweet, the blessed songs,
>   That he to us has given :
> We know he loved us here on earth ;
>   We love him though in heaven.
>
> We love the sparkling 'Golden Chain,
>   The ' Shower' of beauties rare ;
> The ' Censer ' full of joyous praise,
>   ' Fresh Laurels,' green and fair.
> We love to sing his songs of heaven,
>   Of Jesus and His love ;
> They make us happier here below,
>   And raise our thoughts above.

We love the things that he has loved ;
   We love his earthly name ;
And when we know his angel form,
   We'll love him just the same.
We'll love each other better then,
   We'll love ' Our Father ' more ;
We'll roll a sweeter song of praise
   Along the ' Golden Shore.' "

In this little memorial poem the titles of some five or six of Mr. Bradbury's Sunday-school Hymn and Tune Books are thus happily introduced.

Chapter II.

*Teaching in Rome, Pa.—Acquaintance with and Marriage to Lucy Young
—Her Character—Working upon the Farm and Teaching Music—
Letter from Rev. Darwin Cook—Mr. Bliss in his new Home—His
Father's Last Days—" Grandfather's Bible."*

N 1858, when twenty years of age, Mr. Bliss was a
teacher in Rome, Pennsylvania, whither he had
first gone to attend the Musical Convention. A
daguerreotype confirms the descriptions which his
friends give of his appearance at that time. His face is full
of kindliness, frankness, and humour.

Among the pupils in the Academy where he taught was
a Lucy Young, the daughter of a leading citizen in the
valley, and a thrifty farmer, who had married the daughter
of John Allen, also a man of some standing, and of whose
wife we shall hear again. PHILIP BLISS, whose affectionate
nature was always planning for his own family, brought to
the Academy, to pursue her studies under his own eye and
provision, his youngest sister. Lucy Young, at that time
about eighteen years of age, formed a strong attachment to
this sister. They became inseparable friends, and the
brother discovered that one of the companions had become
to him more than a friend. Her quiet, firm, artistic, and
devout nature was the complement of his own more impul-
sive and buoyant one.

On a beautiful summer day, about a year after, the two,

accompanied by those who loved them, went down the lovely valley of the Wysochen, and were united in the holiest of bonds by the pastor in his own dwelling. Singing birds filled the air with music on that June morning, and brooks murmured sweet sounds, as the two lovers of music and song rode to their wedding. Little did they think that, eighteen years after, amid the sweeter songs of angels, the two would go hand in hand within the pearly gates.

Welcome was given to the musical teacher by the family of the bride. He continued his labours, however, on the farm, and on the day of his marriage laid aside his bridal suit to follow his daily toil. In his diary he wrote :—" June 1st, 1859. Married to Miss Lucy J. Young ; the very best thing I could have done." He never, in his deep thankfulness, kept back how much he owed to her. One sentence, written in 1874, is repeated in various forms all through those years —" We are well, happy, cheerful, content." Health and sickness, joy and sorrow, were theirs ; but he always found a moral support in the wife of his youth. At sixteen years of age she had avowed her love to Christ, and her piety sustained his. She was practical, wise, thoughtful, and highly musical.

In 1860 a Normal Academy of Music was held in Geneseo, New York, under Perkins, Cook, Bassini, and others. It was the great event of the period among the musical people of the surrounding country. The advantages offered were of the utmost value to those desiring to cultivate music. Philip Bliss obtained the programme, and eagerly pored over the inducements and opportunities it held out. It was just what he needed. It would be such a joy to him to meet these masters in the art—such a help to him for all the future ; but the expense was far beyond his means. He had not a dollar in the world which he could spare. It seemed impossible for him to go. He was almost heartbroken about it. He threw himself upon the old settee in the sitting-room one day, when no one but Grandma Allen was in the room, and he said, " I just cried from disappointment. I thought everything had come to an end ; that my life must be passed as a farm hand and country teacher, and all bright hopes for the future must be given up." Grandma Allen was his wife's grandmother, and wanted to know all about the trouble. After she had been told of his musical longings, she said,

"Now, Phil., what does that cost? "

"Well, Grandma," he said, "it would take as much as thirty dollars."

"Well, thirty dollars is a good deal of money," said the kind old lady ; "I have an old stocking that I have been dropping pieces of silver in for a good many years, and I'll just see how much there is. Perhaps there are thirty dollars ; and if there are, why, you can take it, and go to the Normal."

The stocking was brought out, and found to contain more than the thirty dollars, and Bliss spent six weeks of the hardest study of his life at the Normal Academy. God bless dear old Grandma Allen ! The world owes her interest compounded a hundred times over as long as she lives, and a grateful remembrance after her death, for what she did that day for her grandson.

Mr. Bliss has been spoken of as a Sunday-school teacher at that time. " Praise Meetings," with careful preparation and what he terms the "two P.'s" of "promptness" and "precision," were services he constantly urged on Sunday-school teachers and churches. The following from his pen is given as characteristic of his spirit and method.

"'How did it go off?' is properly asked of a praise meeting.

"One very important thing is promptness. Do not wait for anybody, or anything. First, ask a blessing. 'My soul, wait thou only upon God; for my expectation is from Him;' then a familiar hymn and tune which all can sing. 'Ariel,' 'Shining Shore,' 'Rock of Ages,' or 'Sweet Hour of Prayer,' will be a good 'send off.' Urge every one to sing as well as may be, but be very careful that no one or two or four sing so well as to separate themselves from the rest. When the sun rises, stars disappear. One who sings a little too well may discourage a dozen. Stimulate the desire to sing rather than urge singing as a duty.

"'Why is ye always a whistlin', Jem?' asked a labouring man of his fellow. 'I whistles to make myself happy,' said he; 'what for do you?' 'I has to whistle 'cause I is happy,' was the reply. How many poor Christians we have seen singing to make themselves happy! how few have to sing because they are happy! Good singing may produce good feeling, but better have the heart right; then good singing, true praise, will be

"'The Christian's vital breath
The Christian's native air.'

"Do not criticise too severely. Many matters of time, tune, etc., will regulate themselves, or, at least, be most improved by being well let alone. And generally, those who sing at all think they sing pretty well; so do not waste time and breath by scolding. If a congregation had a chance to sing oftener, they would sing better.

"The best way to learn to sing is TO SING. Make due allowance for the modesty of such singers as that good old deacon who said he knew his voice was rough and heavy, so in order not to make any discord he always tried to keep a little behind the rest!

"Occasional Scripture texts, illustrations, prayers, etc., will add greatly to the interest of a praise meeting.

" Finally, adjourn before the Meeting is tired. The best time to stop is just when you feel most like going on. So I stop."

He said on another occasion, " Many a good sermon has been like seed blown away, for want of a hearty hymn to harrow it in. Many a prayer-meeting has dragged its slow length along for want of the lubrication of a cheerful praise-spirit in some soul-full song. ' Whoso offereth praise,' says God, ' glorifies me.' "

In these quiet duties of home and school, Mr. Bliss was pleasantly passing his days. There is little remarkable in such a life ; but is it not amid such common-place duties that the great Father best trains his children?. Are not such scenes the school for the growth of humility, considerateness, helpfulness? In such quiet paths is not the habit of piety best developed? At this time Mr. Bliss studied hard, and worked for others unceasingly, and he could write : " How precious is Christ to me to-day ! He has been here in the study all the morning."

It was in the winter of 1860 Mr. Bliss entered upon the profession of music-master. The next three years were spent in the neighbourhood of Rome, Pa. During the winter months his time was fully occupied with teaching; in the summer he worked diligently upon the farm of his father-in-law, using his spare hours in attending the Normal Academy of Music. As superintendent of a Union Sunday-school in the village, his fervency of speech became so marked that he was encouraged by ministers to enter upon the life of an evangelist. His modesty, however, so far held him back. It may be added, his regard for ministers of religion was invariably sincere and cordial. He had no stronger desire than to be helpful to them in their work ; and from no class have so many and such tender expressions of affection for his memory been received as from ministers of the gospel.

In the *Church's Musical Visitor*, Mr. F. W. Root thus wrote of Mr. Bliss :—" He was a poet-musician ; and if ever a man seemed fashioned by the Divine hand for special and exalted work, that man was P. P. Bliss. He had a splendid physique, a handsome face, and a dignified, striking presence. It sometimes seemed incongruous, delightfully so, that in one of such great size and masculine appearance there should also appear such gentleness of manner, such perfect amiability, such conspicuous lack of self-assertion, such considerateness and deference to all, and such almost feminine sensitiveness. He had not had opportunities for large intellectual culture, but his natural mental gifts were wonderful. His faculty for seizing upon the salient features of whatever came under his notice amounted to an unerring instinct. The one kernel of wheat in a bushel of chaff was the first thing he saw. And his ability to control words and phrases so that they should realize a thousand odd conceits of his imagination seemed unlimited. Mr. Bliss's voice was always a marvel to me. He used occasionally to come to my room, requesting that I would look into his vocalization with a view to suggestions. At first a few suggestions were made, but latterly I could do nothing but admire. Beginning with E flat, or even D flat below, he would, without apparent effort, produce a series of clarion tones, in an ascending series, until, having reached the D (fourth line tenor clef), I would look to see him weaken and give up, as would most bass singers ; but no, on he would go, taking D sharp, E, F, *F sharp, and G*, without weakness, without throatiness, without a sound of straining, and without the usual apoplectic look of effort. I feel quite sure in saying that his chest range was from D flat below to A flat above, the quality being strong and agreeable throughout, and one vowel as good as another. He would have made a name and fortune on the dramatic stage."

Mr. and Mrs. Bliss's pastor at that time was the Rev. Darwin Cook. Mr. Cook wrote of him in these terms :—

"About 1855 I first met P. P. Bliss in the church at Rome. He stood in the choir, and sang. In our little company he could not fail to be observed. Therefore I said to Mr. O. F. Young, my chorister, ''That young man's voice is worth a thousand dollars a year. Perhaps he does not know it.' Mr. Young took him home with him to dinner, and afterwards gave him his daughter. Mr. Bliss afterwards said that remark of mine was the first hint he ever received that he had any competency, or any possibilities more than ordinary."

During this period of his life at Rome, he saved up, from the proceeds of his singing schools, a few hundred dollars, and bought a little cottage, to which he removed his parents, and for a time set up housekeeping. The dear old father, who had passed most of his days in humble dwellings in the backwoods, was now sixty-five years of age. The little cottage in Rome was a better home than he had ever lived in. During many months his children, "Phil" and Lucy, had planned the surprise that awaited him. They had saved in every possible way to buy and plainly furnish the little home. When all was made ready, Father Bliss was sent for. The day of his arrival in Rome, he stopped at Father Young's for dinner. In the afternoon, the happy children took the gentle, laughing, grey-haired old Christian in the waggon, and, riding along the one village street, asked him to pick out the house that they had selected to be his home. Two or three times he essayed to express his choice, picking out the humblest, and each time taking a poorer one, until at last he gave up, a little troubled that he might have been too ambitious. The happy " Phil," almost too full to contain himself, turned the team, and, driving back up the street, stopped at a pretty little cottage, a neat piazza in front, a large yard filled with blossoming lilacs and budding apple-trees ; and as the strong man lifted his father from the waggon, it was one of his happiest hours, as he said, " This is your home, father." The dear old man sat down and wept with gratitude to God and to his son.

If Mr. Bliss's father, inheriting Puritan convictions, had occasionally assumed a precise manner, he became from this time happy as a child. The atmosphere he lived in created a perpetual sweetness and serenity about him. The Bible was his one book, and the sense of the reality of eternal things which pervaded the poetry of the son had its origin in the intense convictions of his father. The son watched over him to the end. In 1864 the saintly man passed away, and this chapter cannot be better closed than by the song which Mr. Bliss wrote, into which he has woven, as will be seen, the accompaniment of psalm and song that, in the household, went alongside the reading of the Bible.

> The Sabbath day—sweet day of rest—
>   Was drawing to a close ;
> The summer breeze went murmuring by,
>   To lull me to repose.
> I took my Father's Bible down—
>   His father's gift to him—
> A treasure rare, beyond compare,
>   Though soiled the page, and dim.
>
> " Old friend," said I, " if thou couldst tell,
>   What would thy memories be ? "
> And from the Book there seemed to come
>   This evening reverie :

" Good-will to men ! Peace be to thee !
  My mission aye hath been —
To tell the love of Him who died
  To save a world from sin.

" A hundred years ago I sailed,
  With those who sail no more ;
Through perils dread, by land and sea,
  I reached New England's shore :
There, on a soul-worn, faithful band,
  This soothing psalm did fall :
' Lord, Thou hast been our dwelling-place
  In generations all.'

" Year after year, in temples rude,
  Upon the desk I lay,
To teach of Him, the Great High Priest,
  The Life, the Truth, the Way :
And multitudes who listened there
  To God's life-giving Word,
Are resting from their labours now,
  ' For ever with the Lord.'

" Anon a lowly home I found,
  But love and peace were there ;
The children with the father read,
  And knelt with him in prayer ;
And through the valley, as one passed,
  I heard her sweetly sing :
' O Grave, where is thy victory ?
  O Death, where is thy sting ? '

" Hold fast the faith," the old Book said ;
  " Thy Father's God adore,
And on the Rock of Ages rest
  Thy soul for evermore."
" Amen," said I ; " by grace, I will,
  Till at His feet we fall,
And join the everlasting song,
  And crown Him Lord of all."

Chapter III.

HITHERTO we have seen Philip Bliss as a child of
nature and of God. Mountains, vales, songs of
birds, and the sweet affections of earth had gone
far to form his unartificial character. His path
was bathed in sunshine; and without ambition, or con-
sciousness of remarkable endowments, he used his gifts like
a child who sings and smiles rather from the promptings of
instinct than of purpose and design. He still called himself
"a country boy," and his modesty repaid with generous
affection any small services rendered to him. He wrote his
first little poem, called "Lora Vale," when he was twenty-
six, and was astonished to find that the eminent musical
firm of Messrs. Root and Candy thought it worth publishing
among their sheet music, and more astonished when he
found that the song became popular.

Mr. James McGranahan, a friend and townsman of
Mr. Bliss's, and himself a composer of some repute, thus
records the circumstance : " I well remember Bliss's first
musical composition. He sent the manuscript to Root and
Candy, and after a time he received back a proof *in print*.
He brought in the copy to show me, and to ask my opinion

as to corrections. I had had one or two pieces printed, and knew just how he felt, and we had a very pleasant time over his first piece. It was a great pleasure to him, and yet he felt a great deal of wonder that anything he had written was worth publishing."

There is nothing special in the little poem, but it has a musical and even flow, and an interest attaches to it as being his first production.

LORA VALE.

Calmly fell the silver moonlight
    Over hill and over dale,
As with mournful hearts we lingered
    By the couch of Lora Vale.
She was dying, gentle Lora ;
    She was passing, like a sigh,
From a world of love and beauty
    To a brighter world on high.

Brightly dawned the morrow's morning,
    Over hill and over dale ;
Still with mournful hearts we lingered
    By the side of Lora Vale.
She was almost at the river,
    When the light broke from the sky,
And she smiled and whispered faintly,
    "I am not afraid to die."

Softly through the trellised window
    Came the west wind's gentle breath,
But she heeded not its mildness,
    For she slept the sleep of death ;
And beyond the silver moonbeams,
    Aye, beyond the stars of night,
Now she dwells, our darling Lora,
    In the home of angels bright.

    Lora, Lora, still we love thee,
        Though we see thy form no more ;
    And we know thou'lt come to meet us,
        When we reach the mystic shore.

These simple lines led to Mr. Bliss's introduction to Mr. G. F. Root, of Chicago, and had doubtless an influence in the events that drew him to that energetic city of the West, and that brought him into communion with those evangelistic movements which have drawn to the city the attention of all Christian lands.

"We published 'Lora Vale,'" writes Mr. Root, "and this led to further correspondence. Our interest in him constantly increased. His curious fancies, so piquant and varied, his beautiful penmanship, his bright nature, that did not seem to see anything unhappy or unbeautiful in life, attracted us strongly, and led often to letters on my part that were not needed for business purposes, but were for the sake of the answer they were sure to bring. The deeper nature of the man did not show then, but that which did appear was ' pure, and lovely, and of good report.'

" Whether the proposition to come to Illinois was ' out of the whole cloth ' from us, or whether he intimated, as our correspondence progressed, that he would like to come, I do not remember ; but about 1863 or '64 he did come, and pleasant was our surprise to find that our bright and attractive letter-writer lived in a ' house ' every way worthy of him. It is rare indeed to find both mind and body alike so strong, healthy, and beautiful, in one individual as they were in him. He went to work, first about the State, holding Musical Conventions and giving concerts, and attending to the interests of certain parts of our business ; sending to us occasional communications and compositions for our musical paper. I do not recall particulars about these compositions.· I only know that it was my pleasure to look them over and suggest, if I could, improvements, or hint at faults now and then, especially in the earlier ones. I say ' my pleasure,' for never had teacher so teachable and docile a subject for criticism.

"I do not know of his modes or habits of composition, but I do know of his wonderful fertility and facility. His responses to the calls for the many kinds of literary and musical work that we soon found he could do, always surprised us as much by their promptness as by their uniform excellence. It is probable that with every topic that entered his mind there came trooping multitudes of congruous ideas, images and words, and he had only to take his choice; and his choice was always happy, always appropriate, and often striking in its originality and beauty.

"It was lovely to see how near to all he did was his religion. There was for him no line on one side of which was a bright face and on the other a solemn one. His smile went into his religion and his religion into his smile. His Lord was always welcome, and apparently always there in his open and loving heart. It was this that made his liveliness so irresistibly sweet and attractive. You constantly felt its sphere of innocence. This hymn, by a kindred spirit, is a most true expression of his constant condition :—

" ' Thy happy ones a strain begin ;
Dost not Thou, Lord, glad souls possess ?
Thy cheerful spirit dwells within ;
We feel Thee in our joyfulness.

Our mirth is not afraid of Thee,
Our life rejoices to be bright ;
We would not from our gladness flee,
We give full welcome to delight.

Thou wilt not, Lord, our smiles deny ;
Dost Thou not deem them of rich worth ?
Our cheer flows on beneath Thine eye ;
We feel accepted in our mirth.

We turn to Thee a smiling face,
Thou sendest us a smile again ;
Our joy the richness of Thy grace,
Thine own, the cheer of this glad strain.' "

Should not this be the order with which we receive the gifts of our loving God?—first, response to His heavenly striving; then, asking; then, hoping; then, believing; and then, confidence, praise, gladness. "The kingdom of God is . . . righteousness, and peace, and joy in the Holy Ghost" (Rom. xiv. 17).

His glad heart gave birth to songs which he caught from the most unlikely scenes and sounds of nature. A little poem which he wrote for children may be quoted in illustration :—

BEAUTIFUL RAIN.

Hear the music of the rain falling down,
On the roof and window pane, falling down.
　"Murmur not," it seems to say,
　"For our Father's love to-day
　Orders only in our way
　　Good to fall."
Like the gentle falling rain
Over mountain, lake, and plain,
Will His tender care remain
　　Over all.

　　Hear the music of the rain, beautiful rain,
　　　As the pearly drops in showers pattering fall ;
　　Hear the sweet subdued refrain,
　　On the roof and window pane,
　　　Of our Father's tender love for all.

Hear the music of the rain falling down,
On the roof and window pane, falling down ;
　What a lesson does it bring !
　What a chorus does it sing !
　What a message from our King,
　　Of His love.
And we seem to hear Him say—
"Come, ye children, learn My way,
From My fold no longer stray ;
　　Look above !"

Hear the music of the rain falling down,
On the roof and window pane, falling down :
    So our Father, kind and true,
    Showers of blessings, ever new,
    Over the good and evil, too,
        Still doth send ;
    And a cheerful song we raise,
    To His honour and His praise,
    For the love that crowns our days
        To the end.

His advocacy for the singing of children thus expresses itself:—

"All know that children *love* to sing. Next after the adoption of a resolution that the birds 'can and are hereby authorized to warble,' may come the question of granting the children—God's own bright birds of Paradise—permission to express *their* delights in song."

Is the question asked, "What shall the children sing? Unquestionably we cannot be too careful to guard against putting a cup of poisoned song to their youthful lips, and yet I cannot sympathize with those who would have only doctrinal, didactic, dogmatic songs, or rather sermons. If a child really sings, he must not only fully understand, but *love* the meaning of the words employed."

The idea, however, which Mr. Bliss had of the use of Sacred Song is thus indicated in an address he gave at a State Sunday School Association:—"Let song develop feeling, and then do not fail to use the feeling to direct and purify affection." The utterance is singularly wise, and deserves to be remembered in England. Hymns in Sunday-schools and social meetings are often used for the sake of the enjoyment they afford, and not with an ulterior object. It is a great loss and mistake when evoked feeling is not used to guide the conscience and to win the heart. Men there are who

never cultivate emotion, and never indulge in it, and who
would be glad to think that the heart can be reached
through the head, and that intellect sways the affections.
But it is not so. "The ennobling difference," says Mr.
Ruskin, "between one man and another—between one
animal and another—is precisely in this, that one feels
more than another : we are only human in so far as we are
sensitive, and our honour is precisely in proportion to our
passion." *

Mr. Bliss now began to conduct the music in General
Associations of Ministers. He says of one—"There was
much fine talking, a few earnest prayers, but very little
hearty singing. Would not singing improve hearts as well
as voices? But please don't put me down as fault-finding."
The last phrase is characteristic of the man. In the same
communication he speaks of a young lady named Kate
Cameron, in whose religious welfare he had been interested,
and who received the welcome to the Church above on the
same day she was to have been united to the Church below.
She wrote these words, among others equally striking :—

> You tell me of a city
>   That is so bright and fair ;
> Oh, why do not the friends I love
>   Talk more of going there?

Mr. Bliss's occupation was at this time that of holding
Musical Conventions, and giving private instruction in music
in towns through the north-west. First his Conventions were
held under arrangement with Messrs. Root and Candy, and
after that by independent appointment. He was very popular
as a musical conductor and teacher. Mrs. Bliss frequently
accompanied her husband, and assisted with her voice in
his Conventions. Every summer they returned to Rome

* " Sesame and Lilies."

to visit the old homestead. It was there among the hills and during the home-rest that he wrote many of his sweetest pieces.

At the close of this year he writes in his diary : " Thus the overruling providence of God has led me by unmistakable evidences to see and recognize His dealing with me all through life's journey. Truly we have much to be thankful for. My dear wife, my greatest earthly treasure, joins in the opinion that we are, and ever have been, highly favoured of Heaven. We find our greatest enjoyment in each other's society, when striving to make each other happy ; and our highest aim is to be useful to ourselves and others, and to ' glorify God that we may enjoy Him for ever.' "

The sentiment of gratitude that ever actuated Mr. Bliss is shown in these lines. His first impulse, in every good thing that came to him, and in all his joy and happiness— sometimes arising from what appeared to others comparatively trifling causes—was to fall on his knees and thank God. The sentiment of deep attachment to his wife that pervaded his life is also shown. They were indeed inseparable ; fond of each other, and helpful to each other in all the intercourse of life. May the example of these dear friends in this respect be owned of God to make more happy Christian homes where the relation of husband and wife fails to reach its deepest significance because it is not sanctified in Christ.

It was in 1869 that the event occurred which Mr. Bliss regarded as the most important in his life : this was his meeting with, and forming the acquaintance of, Mr. D. L. Moody. Mr. Moody was holding Gospel services in Wood's Museum, near the corner of Randolph and Clark Streets, in Chicago. For half an hour preceding his meeting in the theatre of the museum, he was in the habit of speaking in the open air from the steps of the Court

House near by.   Mr. Bliss has told of this meeting as
follows :—

   " I had been nearly four years in the West at that
time, and had passed a good many Sundays in Chicago,
returning from the country where I was occupied holding Musical Conventions ; but I had never met Mr.
Moody.   One Sunday evening, my wife and I went out
for a walk before going to church, and passing up Clark
Street we came upon the open-air meeting.   I was at
once attracted by the earnestness of the speaker, who, I
was told, was Moody, and, waiting until he closed with an
earnest appeal for all to follow him to the theatre, we decided we would go, and fell in with the crowd, and spent
the evening in his meeting there.   That night Mr. Moody
was without his usual leader for the singing, and the music
was rather weak.   From the audience I helped what I
could on the hymns, and attracted the evangelist's attention.
At the close of the meeting, he was at the door shaking
hands with all who passed out, and as I came to him he
had my name and history in about two minutes, and a promise that when I was in Chicago on Sunday evenings, I
would come and help in the singing at the theatre meetings.
This was the commencement of our acquaintance.   I sang
at the theatre meetings often after that, and, making longer
stops in Chicago in connection with writing music, I was
often at the noon meeting, and was frequently made use of
by Mr. Moody in his various gatherings."

   "Where in the world has such a man been kept," asked
Mr. Moody, "that he has not before become known in
Chicago?   To think that such a singer should have been
around here for the last four years, and we working here for
Christ have not known him."   Ah, it is often thus : men
whose native modesty keeps them in the background, are
passed over for the sake of others who press to the front.

Paul retired to Tarsus after his vision of the Lord. Barnabas went to fetch him thence, when he saw " the grace of God " so manifested in the Syrian Antioch, and when he needed such a helper. The record finely shows how the one waited till Christ called him to the work by His providence, and ' how the other was eager to introduce to the Church a helper who could advance its perfecting and enlargement.

The meeting of Mr. Bliss and Mr. Moody constituted an epoch. We may glance for a moment at the service to which they were called.

If in the vast sheep-walks of Australia a dozen shepherds had the care of many thousands of sheep, and should be debating about the shape and colour of their own attire, the construction of their tents, the form of their folds, or even discussing, in loyalty to their master, arrangements for the well-being of their flocks, and at the same time were doing nothing effectual towards bringing back a larger number of strayed sheep than those that were folded, the master-shepherd would probably appoint special men to restore the wanderers. It would be the wisdom of the shepherds not to look on such men as doing an unauthorized work, but to co-operate with them. There is scarcely a more pathetic figure than that used in the Gospel of Matthew, where it is recorded that our Lord had compassion on the multitude because they were as sheep scattered abroad, having no shepherd." To an onlooker no sight could be more affecting than that of poor, witless, helpless sheep, exposed on all sides to ravenous beasts, and which were unshepherded.

This is the special labour to which the Great Friend and Divine Brother of our race has been summoning His servants in these last days. To a man like Mr. Moody, with great natural force, common-sense convictions, a vigour of utterance occasionally touching genius, and with remarkably clear views of the Gospel of God's love, no service could seem more imperative than to arrest the attention of the growing and countless throngs of men who were given up to business, pleasure, or grossness, without a ray of light as to their eternal destiny and their need of salvation. There were three links in the chain of influence whereby he sought to overtake this ever-augmenting ungodliness. The first was personal visitation of Christian men and women from house to house ; the last was personal contact of believers with anxious ones in the inquiry room ; the intermediate one was an attractive religious service, unprofessional, informal, and baptized with prayer.

From the time Mr. Moody met with Mr. Bliss, dates his impression of the power of solo-singing in these evangelistic labours. At all events, such impressions as he had were crystallized at that time. Singing as an enjoyment was not the end that was sought. Why should it be thought strange that singing by a man of taste, rich emotion, and musical ability, should soften the heart, and, by God's blessing, break the hard crust of worldliness that may have gathered over the soul ? If the voice of powerful speaking can arouse the conscience and touch the heart-chords, why may not singing do the same ? That the thing is novel in our age can be no objection. The singing of sacred songs through English villages in the time of the Lollards broke the darkness of the Middle Ages, and was the precursor of the Reformation.* That the feeling evoked is often transient,

* Nor was it singing only that so touched the heart of English people at that time. The Rev. Stopford Brooke says, in his "English Literature," that the poem of "Piers the Ploughman" wrought so strongly in men's minds that its influence was almost as great as Wycliff's, in the revolt which had begun against Latin Christianity.

is no more than what all preachers deplore ; the deeper the
emotion, the more lamentable is the "passing away."

It is quite true that singing the Gospel can be abused
by pretenders. But is not preaching? It is true that men
are not to be charmed out of their sins by song. But if
our theologies are not revealing Christ's love, who will object
if the poor followers of this world's pleasures are thrilled by
the sweetness of a heavenly strain, and if the crushed
victims of our modern ways are touched by a new melodious
voice which interprets to them the Divine Shepherd's call?
It was not singing alone that Mr. Bliss advocated and Mr.
Moody adopted. It was singing as an auxiliary to verbal
teaching, and as a preparation for the testimony of the
speaker, or of the wise instructor in the inquiry room.

Altogether, we may affirm that the vivid impression of the
power of Christian song which Mr. Moody received when he
heard Mr. Bliss, forms an epoch in the history of a movement that has been among the most blessed and remarkable
in modern times, and has more or less changed the nature
of religious meetings in all parts of Christendom. Thus
Mr. Bliss wrote of this work :—

"This singing and talking about the Good News of a
present, perfect, free salvation and justification by faith is
so popular and attractive, I do not believe I shall ever find
time for anything else. It seems to me it is needed. How
much of everything else we hear preached, and how little
Gospel!"

It was soon after this that Mr. Bliss met with Major
Whittle in Chicago. The two faithful and consecrated men
were as brothers from that hour ; they laboured together in
the gospel, and the latter has furnished the materials from
which the English editor has compiled this narrative. Major
Whittle took Mr. Bliss to his house, No. 43, South Street.
The Major records, "Very sacred is the memory of those

days. How kind and tender was dear Bliss to my invalid
father ! How he would cheer him in his joyous, hearty way
by singing his favourite songs ! A noble, manly young man
was also there, who has since passed into glory. What precious seasons had we of family worship ! What interesting
Bible discussions, and talk over Sunday schools ! How was Mr.
Bliss at all times the same kind-hearted and loveable man !"

It was there in that residence, and at that time, that Mr.
Bliss wrote the song and music of his " I am so glad that
Jesus loves me," and of that martial strain familiar now to
hundreds of thousands, "Hold the Fort." Mr. Root
says :—" 'Hold the Fort' was written upon an incident
familiar to all, which occurred in our civil war. I consider
this work an extraordinary combination of effects, a striking
cluster of pure gems of sentiment. The first element in it
is an appeal to love of country ; our patriotism stirs mightily
within us as we read of the gallant struggles of our soldiers
at Altoona Pass—of their heroic endurance and final deliverance by General Sherman. Mr. Bliss's strong, epigrammatic
poem, crystallizes the parallel, and points it with Gospel
truth that it may strike home to every hearer. The pictures,
however they be considered from a technical standpoint,
stimulate the imagination to a more vivid apprehension of
the allegory, and then comes the music touching the whole
with Promethean fire, and giving it wings that it may fly to
the uttermost parts of the earth, and to the innermost
recesses of the soul. A man must be without patriotic
enthusiasm, without religious sentiment, and without æsthetic
sensibility, who can look upon this work unmoved."

In the year 1870 the First Congregational Church of
Chicago, having just gone into a handsome ecclesiastical
structure at the corner of Washington Street, desired a
choir-master. Mr. Bliss was appointed to the position.

Mr. and Mrs. Bliss became members of the church and remained so till they were lifted up to the perfected church. The following record of Mr. Bliss in this new character, which has been contributed by his pastor, the Rev. Dr. Goodwin, is too valuable to be curtailed.*

"In July, 1870, Mr. Bliss became leader of the choir of my First Congregational Church of Chicago, and a few months later, the superintendent of the Sabbath school. He continued to hold both of these positions for something more than three years, resigning his superintendency only when he had fairly entered upon his work as a singing evangelist. As may be supposed, I saw him very often during all this period, and came to know him well; and the memory of the friendship that grew up between us, and interlocked our hearts more and more as the fellowship of worship and work went on, is and will ever be a perpetual joy. His was a nature to invite confidence and to keep it. Thoroughly frank and unsuspecting, with not a thought of policy or craft, intensely sympathetic and outspoken, with a heart overflowing with kindness of spirit, a conscience quick to hear and imperative to heed every call of duty, a devotion to the service of the Master that never seemed to falter or grow cold, he drew me to him from the first as a brother and yoke-fellow to be exceedingly beloved and rejoiced in ; and the better I knew him the more I admired the unaffected simplicity and beauty of his character—the more I felt impressed with the depth and earnestness of his piety —the more I leaned upon and valued his co operation.

"Few pastors, I am persuaded, are privileged to have

---

* Dr. Goodwin's remarks have no doubt a special application to the state of things in the United States. But they will not be without their use and appropriateness to churches on this side the Atlantic.

in their choristers such gifted, sympathizing, efficient helpers.
Too often, it is to be feared, the pulpit and the choir
gallery are out of harmony as to the ends proposed, or the
methods by which the ends agreed on shall be sought; and
the cases are not few, nor hard to find, where, in the hand-
ling of choir leaders and those who abet them, the Lord's
house is turned into a concert hall, the service of song
made largely a device for filling and renting pews, and the
minister compelled to sandwich his part in between per-
formances that suggest anything but the worship of God or
the salvation of men. Sometimes, indeed, he has to come
to his duties in the pulpit after the world and the flesh and
the devil have, through the fingers and lips of an uncon-
verted organist and choir leader, set things moving to their
liking, and then turn the service over to them after the
sermon, to be finished up as they may elect. Doubtless the
devil likes that way of conducting Sabbath services. If
he can only get people's heads full of waltzes, operas,
sonatas, and what-not else, before the preaching comes, and
then have a chance to follow it up with a 'march' or an 'aria'
of his own selection, the preacher's thirty minutes of gospel
will not greatly damage his interests. Little wonder that
preaching in such circumstances saves few souls. It is like
expecting harvest with the enemy invited to go before the
toiler sowing tares, and to follow him gathering up and
snatching away the seed.

" To those who knew anything of P. P. Bliss, it will not
be needful to say that he had no sympathy with any such
idea of the music of the sanctuary. He shared to the
fullest extent my feeling, that the disposition to make the
song and service of God's house showy and entertaining was
an abomination in God's sight. He held, as I did, that all
music in connection with worship, whether by instrument or
voice, should be consecrated and worshipful. In his con-

ception, he who led at the organ should be one to come to
the keys fresh from his closet—one who should pray, as his
hands swept over the manuals, that the power of God
might, through him, constrain the people's hearts to worship
in spirit and in truth. So he believed that all who led in
the service of song should sing with grace in their hearts ;
that the music should be strictly spiritual music—not selections made on grounds of taste, high musical character ; but
selections aimed at honouring God, exalting Jesus Christ,
magnifying His Gospel—music, in a word, that God's Spirit
could wholly own and use to comfort, strengthen, and
inspire God's people, and lead unsaved souls to Christ.
Accordingly the highest devotional character marked all his
selections, all his rehearsals, all his leadership in the Lord's
house. It was his invariable custom to open his rehearsals
by prayer. He often invited me to lead in that service, and
to address the choir on the subject of the singing adapted to
worship ; and few weeks passed without his impressing the
spiritual idea as the all-controlling one, and one never to be
forgotten by those who were to lead the praises of the congregation.

"Many times during rehearsals he would say, 'When
we sing, let us forget everything but the cross. Let us
seek to have the people lose sight of us, of our efforts, our
skill, and think only of Him who died thereon, and of the
peace, comfort, strength, joy, He gives them that trust Him.'
It is not strange that, with such a choir-leader in charge,
all solicitude about 'anthems' and 'voluntaries' vanished
from the preacher's mind. Whatever the selection, I knew
it would be full of worship alike in the sentiment and the
rendering, and would prepare the way for the Word of God ;
and when the sermon was ended, no matter what the final
thought, whether admonition, encouragement, or appeal, I
always felt sure that the chorister's heart was one with mine,

and that I could commit the closing service to him, as I sometimes did, with perfect confidence that the impression sought to be produced would be deepened.

"This was pre-eminently true of Mr. Bliss's management of the singing in all gatherings for prayer. He was a royal helper here. He loved such fellowship, could not bear to have things drag and grow listless and stupid, as they sometimes do. His sunny, buoyant nature could not tolerate such an atmosphere, his warm, fresh feelings brought him at once to the rescue. He would break out at such times with one of his ringing songs that would go through all hearts like the blast of a bugle, and set everything astir. He was especially fond of songs that magnified the name and grace of Christ, and urged to larger trust and consecration and engagedness in His service. 'Free from the Law,' 'More Holiness give me,' 'I gave My Life for Thee,' 'The Half was never Told,' 'Hold fast till I Come,' were among his favourites, and they would sometimes scatter the gloom and despondency, or the coldness of a Meeting, as a sudden burst of sunshine through a thick sky puts to rout clouds and fog. Indeed, a stupid, lifeless Meeting with P. P. Bliss in it would have been a marvel. All through his songs and his words of witness breathed the spirit of absorbing devotion.

"With him the 'coming of the Lord' was a Scripture truth, so real and vivid that his life felt the inspiration of it in everything he said or did. He felt profoundly that the Bridegroom might come at any moment, and hence it was his intense desire to have his work done, his lamp trimmed, and to be ready to enter in to the marriage. During the last two years while engaged as an Evangelist, he was rarely present in the prayer-meetings; but whenever he was there, almost invariably before he spoke or sang, he gave expression to the feeling that possibly he might be witnessing for the last time. The very last evening when he met with us, he came forward near the close of the meeting, uttering this thought, sang as a word of counsel and encouragement to all young converts, a number of whom had been testifying during the evening, the song whose chorus is :—

> " ' Hold fast till I come,
> Hold fast till I come ;
> A bright crown awaits thee ;
> Hold fast till I come.'

" In his Sunday-school relations, he was especially happy and beloved. It is safe to say that no school ever had a Superintendent who held larger place in the children's hearts than he ; and it is easy to see why. He was an enthusiastic lover of children. It never cost him any effort to meet children on their level, for he lived there. He knew a child's nature by instinct, or rather he possessed such a nature, and could no more help gathering about him, wherever he was, the little four and five-year olds of the infant class, and talking to them in a way that every one of them understood, than a florist could help gathering roses and japonicas and fuchsias about him, and looking at them day by day. And the same with older children. The consequence was, that whenever he appeared before the school, every face brightened instantly. Every eye was intent, every ear eager. He never had to ring for order while he was talking ; never had any rough, turbulent boys whom he could not interest and control. The look of his eye, the sound of his voice, was all-potent.

" The members of his school, young and old, felt him to be a personal friend, and so he was. He knew very many of them by name. He entered keenly into all their childish experiences ; was always ready to listen to the unbosomings which they were eager to pour into his ears; to answer their questions and give the counsel they sought. It was marvellous to see how completely and without effort he possessed their confidence, and how supremely he swayed them by his opinion. Whatever he said was 'law' and 'gospel' in the fullest sense: and whenever he went, as it was his delight to go, among the children's homes, especially those of the humbler sort, in times of sickness, his sunny presence, cheery words, and stirring songs, were better than all medicines. Patience, courage, hopefulness, always followed his visits; and parents were as glad to see him as were the children, and often as much helped by his coming.

"Mr. Bliss's ability to teach children to sing was amazing, and it was compensation for a long pilgrimage to see him handle a school when training it musically. From the moment he named a piece, he seemed to inspire all with his enthusiasm. Not an eye would wander, not a face be dull. He would say a few pithy words, explaining the sentiment of the song, a few more, possibly, about the music and how to render it; sing a strain or two alone, and then, after two or three repetitions, the school would march through and ring it out as if they had been familiar with it for months. It was as if he had the gift of infusing music into everybody. No matter how little musical culture or skill teachers and scholars had, no matter how out of key or out of time, they were naturally inclined to sing. Somehow when Mr. Bliss led, the difficulties and irregularities and discords seemed to disappear, and there was one grand thrill of feeling, one royal burst of harmony.

"The best thing about this singing was that, unlike that of the choir gallery, it was never for show. Mr. Bliss would have abominated any attempt at musical display, or anything simply entertaining, as truly on the part of children as

of adults. With him the Sunday school and all the depart-
ments and appliances of it meant—salvation. He believed
with his whole heart in the early conversion of children.
He was wont to say that he could never remember the time
when he did not trust in Christ as his Saviour and desire to
serve Him. He felt profoundly that when Jesus said
'Suffer the little children to come unto Me and forbid them
not, for of such is the kingdom of heaven,' He meant to
have parents and all understand that He was the children's
Saviour, and that in their tenderest years the little ones
might know renewing grace and become the children of the
Kingdom. He greatly coveted such early trust in Christ,
and with increasing devotion brought to bear all the agencies
at his command to secure it. Next to the Word of God,
he felt the instrumentality of song to be most potent, and he
used it mightily. Praying before he sang, praying while he
sang, and exhorting all others to sing prayerfully and in the
spirit, he led the school. Many times he would stop in the
middle of a song to lift up the cross, emphasize the love of
Jesus, and urge every heart to immediate decision on the
Lord's side. He often did it with tears—tears in his eyes
and tears in his voice; and time and again, as, with that
wonderful pathos and sweetness of which he was such a
master, he poured forth his soul in the affectionate entreaties
of 'Calling Now,' or 'Almost Persuaded,' all hearts would
melt as if touched of God, and the solemn hush that
followed seemed like a moment of universal prayer and
consecration.

" God richly blessed this dear brother's songs and labours
in the school. During his connection with it there was rarely
a communion season without some of its members coming
forward to unite with the church ; and if the names of all
whom he helped by word and song to accept Jesus Christ
as Saviour, while he was Superintendent, could be called,

there would rise up a great cloud of witnesses. Doubtless much of the seed sown proved like that in the parable, seed by the wayside, in stony ground, or among thorns, and came to nought. But there was left, nevertheless, a generous portion that brought forth, some thirty, some sixty, some an hundred fold; and among the children the harvest from his sowing is only begun.

"We saw but little of Mr. Bliss after he entered upon his work as an Evangelist, but what we did see made us all feel that more and more the Spirit of anointing was upon him. Whenever he could, he came back for a visit to the old place of toil and prayer, and never without stirring all our hearts by some word of cheer, or of incitement to larger devotion in the Master's service. Often he would set the blood bounding by a new song rendered as only he could do it; and very likely he would follow this with a prayer, whose child-like simplicity, and earnestness, and pathos, revealed how intimate his communion was with God, and how he longed to be more and more used in winning souls. It is not too much to say that during these last years Christ was in all his thoughts; as one of his later songs expresses it :—

My only song and story,
    Is—Jesus died for me ;
My only hope of glory—
    The cross of Calvary.

"Would that the spirit of such a discipleship might pervade all our singers, our Sunday-school Superintendents, our teachers, our church members ! Then there would be singing in the Spirit, praying in the Spirit, working in the Spirit, and heaven would be kept jubilant over souls rescued from sin. May God help all who read the record of this consecrated life to enter into the secret of its joy and its power—to be determined not to know anything among men save Jesus Christ and Him crucified.

"E. P. GOODWIN."

With two quotations from his letters, we close this chapter. To his mother he writes :—

"You will find in a box sent to Towanda, a black dress. Won't we have a good re-union, when we all get home to heaven ! I do want to see 'Pa Bliss,' and Reliance—Jamie, and the blessed JESUS ! *

"'Truth is : the mercy and favour of Our Father in Heaven seem continually shining on us, unworthy and unthankful as we are. Oh, how we ought to praise and love Him ! Help us !"

To his brother and sister :—

"12, SOUTH ELIZABETH STREET, CHICAGO,
May 24, 1873.

"SWEET SPIRITS,—Tried and true, worthy brother and sister ; our partners in the everlasting inheritance.

"Yes, indeed, the Lord has blessed 'Sunshine' † greatly. Help us to praise Him for it. It is His book anyhow, and He should have the praise.

"The 'Paul' boy is in his usual spirits—gay and blissful. Next Sunday, I think, he will put on his best (McGranahan's) robes and be baptized.

"My joy is full. The Sunday-school prosperous ; thirty joined the church last Sunday. We are in our new base-

---

* "Pa Bliss" was his favourite name for his beloved father. Reliance and Jamie were his brother and sister, both of whom died in 1847.

† "SUNSHINE" was a Hymn and Tune Book then recently published by Mr. Bliss.

ment. Kate Cameron died last week. We sang her own hymn, 'That City,' from 'Joy,' at her funeral.* May we all follow her ! AMEN."

---

*Kate Cameron is named in a preceding chapter. (See page 36.) The hymn "That City," by her, was published in a Tune Book edited by Mr. Bliss, characteristically entitled by him "The Joy." Miss Cameron's hymn is here given :—

THAT CITY.

1 You tell me of a City
　Which is so bright and fair ;
Oh, why do not the friends I love
　Talk more of going there?
I hear them speak of pleasures
　Which earthly things have given;
Why do they never mention
　The better joys of heaven?

A City which hath foundations,
　Whose builder and maker is God,
　　Which shineth afar,
　　Like a beautiful star,
By saints and angels trod.

2 I think about that City
　Of which I have been told,

Whose gates are made of shining
　　pearl,
　Whose streets are paved with
　　gold.
The firm and strong foundation
　Is built of jewels rare ;
I'm sure that nothing earthly
　Can with those walls compare.

3 Oh, dear and blessèd City !
　Could I but enter in,
I should be free from every pain,
　From care, and doubt, and sin.
Oh, let me bear each trial
　As patient as I may,
For soon will all things mortal
　For ever pass away.

Chapter IX.

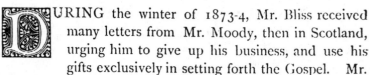URING the winter of 1873-4, Mr. Bliss received many letters from Mr. Moody, then in Scotland, urging him to give up his business, and use his gifts exclusively in setting forth the Gospel. Mr. and Mrs. Bliss were ready to do this, if they could see it as the call of God. Mrs. Bliss's characteristic remark was : " I am willing that Mr. Bliss should do anything that we can be sure is the Lord's will, and I can trust the Lord to provide for us, but I do not want him to take such a step simply on Mr. Moody's will." There was much prayer and much hesitation on Mr. Bliss's part in approaching a decision upon the matter. He doubted his ability to be useful in the work ; doubted whether the drawing he felt toward it was of the Lord, or of his own inclination. Mr. Moody continued to write. One of his sentences was : " You have not faith. If you have not faith of your own on this matter, start out on my faith. Launch out into the deep." A solemn providence of God that occurred at this time, deeply impressed Mr. Bliss. In November, 1874, a Christian brother and dear personal friend, Mr. H. G. Spafford,

received a telegram from England, announcing the drowning
of his four dear children in the loss of the " Ville de Havre."
The telegram contained the two words, "Saved alone."
His wife, who accompanied the children, had been rescued,
and sent the despatch. These friends were dear to Mr.
Bliss, and their affliction was a deep personal sorrow.
Mr. Spafford himself joined in urging the counsel of Mr.
Moody.

It was about this time that the Rev. C. M. Saunders
invited Mr. Bliss and Major Whittle to go to Waukegan,
Illinois, to conduct Meetings for three or four evenings.
Mr. Bliss, to learn better the Lord's will, thus wrote :—

"DEAR BROTHER SAUNDERS,—We are coming to you.
Pray for the Spirit's power to accompany the effort. Every
time you think of our coming, offer a prayer that it may be
for God's glory."

The first evening there was no marked result.
Although it rained hard, the meeting on the second
evening was twice as large. As Mr. Bliss sang his own
"Almost Persuaded," with a heart yearning to bring
wavering ones to decision for Christ, the impression was so
irresistible that many arose while he sang, unable to with-
hold their craving for the help of prayer. That night
there was the joy in Waukegan of those who had come to
Christ with full purpose of heart, and had found the new
bliss of accepting His love. The hearts of the three men
of God who had entered on the work were deeply awed.
" The next afternoon," says one of them, " we all three met
in the vestry of the Congregational Church, where our
Meetings were held, and spent some hours in prayer. Mr.
Bliss made a formal surrender of everything to the Lord ;
gave up his Musical Conventions ; his writing of secular

music; gave up everything, and in a simple, child-like, trusting prayer, he placed himself, with any talent, any power God had given him, at the disposal of the Lord. Major Cole united with us in this consecration. It was a wonderful afternoon. As I think back upon the scene in that little vestry, and recall Bliss's prayer, and the emotions that filled us all in the sense of God's presence, the room seems lit up in my memory with a halo of glory.

"This Consecration Meeting was followed by a wonderful gathering in the evening. Some twenty or more accepted Christ, and a spirit of deep conviction was upon many souls. We returned to Chicago in the morning, praising God—Bliss to find substitutes for his Conventions, and I to resign my business position. From that Wednesday, March 25th, 1874, up to December 15th, 1876, when I parted from him no more to meet on earth, I never heard Mr. Bliss express a regret that he made this surrender, that he gave himself to God for His work."

At this point we may fitly introduce Mr. Bliss's Consecration Hymn, which he called " MY PRAYER."

More holiness give me,
  More strivings within,
More patience in suffering,
  More sorrow for sin,
More faith in my Saviour,
  More sense of His care,
More joy in His service,
  More purpose in prayer.

More gratitude give me,
  More trust in the Lord,
More pride in His glory,
  More hope in His Word,
More tears for His sorrows,
  More pain at His grief,
More meekness in trial,
  More praise for relief.

More purity give me,
  More strength to o'ercome,
More freedom from earth-stains,
  More longings for home.
More fit for the kingdom,
  More used would I be,
More blessed and holy,
  More, Saviour, like Thee.

" His income from his business at this time was good and growing. A few months before this he had said in a letter to a friend, which is preserved, 'I have had an offer to become a conductor of the Handel and Haydn Society of San Francisco, at a salary of 3,000 dollars in gold.' This was for one appointment. His reputation as a composer was increasingly recognized, and he looked forward with his wife to being in a condition where he could settle down and be at home, giving up his Convention work. His decision involved the giving up of income, the simple trusting God for all means of support, the relinquishing of plans for settling down in a home, the lowering of his reputation in the eyes of many well-meaning musical friends, and the taking up of a calling in which it is not possible for one to abide unless laborious and self-denying.

" None of these things that he gave up did Bliss ever speak of. He was as silent about them, just as the disciples in the Gospels, when, with their eyes on the Lord, they followed Him over Palestine, silent about the boats, nets, and fishes they left by the Sea of Galilee. I think Bliss truly counted these things nothing compared with the joy of being a servant of Jesus Christ, and the gladness of being used to impart life by the Gospel to dead souls. On our way to Waukegan, he selected a verse which, said he, ' let us keep, as our watchword in the work.' The verse is in Heb. xii. 2 : ' Looking unto Jesus, the Author and Finisher of our faith ; who, for the joy that was set before

Him, endured the cross, despising the shame, and is set down at the right hand of the throne of God.' His joyous utterance of the 'Looking unto Jesus' chased away fear, and breathed courage into our hearts."

We quote one or two of his letters written at this period. All were fresh and cheery.

To his mother he says: "You may be sure we shall pray for you, and I never can forget that you prayed for me and watched over me many years before I could pray for myself. I love to make mention of praying parents in my prayers and conversation. I feel the strength every day of the early religious training and surroundings—just as a man must be benefited all his lifetime by youthful physical exercise. I am determined the godly ancestry shall not stop with me, but that Paul shall be the subject of much prayer. He shall inherit a good fortune of faith, even if his worldly goods can be tied up in a cotton handkerchief, as mine were when I started for Troy."

To his sister he writes: "We should think of Jesus when we pray, as a dear Friend really listening to us and ready to aid, not as some great Power to be dreaded. So let us come with boldness, liberty, freedom, believing His word and hoping in His mercy. He likes to have us come in earnest, as the poor blind men came, saying, ' Lord, if Thou wilt,' and then He is ready to say, ' I will.' "

Again to his mother he says: " I can testify to you that this life of service to Him who hath bought us is a very delightful one. My cup of joy has always been full, but in these glorious Meetings it often runs over. I am thankful for a wife who can enter into and share the joy of Christian consecration and service. Of course it is the greatest trial of our lives, so far, to be separated so much, but it seems to me especially hard for her.   Nevertheless, the Lord has given her a cheerful heart, and she is just as content and reconciled as any one could be ; says she would not detain me if she could, and prays, oh, so earnestly, for my success and safety.   Again I thank God for a praying wife and a praying mother.   What should I have been but for both ? The Lord only knows.   Last evening two girls came up to me to ' talk religion,' *just in fun !*   It was a painful sight ; my heart was grieved—the Holy Spirit, oh, how much more !   This morning one of them came to prayer meeting and spoke of it with grief and penitence.   One of the first families has a ' high-toned ' girl who has not spoken to her father for three years !   She is asking prayer ; but we said to her this morning, ' How can you ask prayer ? how can you pray with such a heart ? '   Scores are being converted— hopefully, joyfully, scripturally converted.   Praise ye the Lord ! "

To his nephew he writes : " Of the work here I will only say, for the first week it is better, apparently, than in any other place we have ever been in.   Yet this is a German city —a phlegmatic people—a very ' hard place.'   But so much the more need of work ; so much the more honour to Christ in the victory.   Four Meetings daily, and from twenty to forty professing Christ every day.   The Jews are growing more and more approachable and tender, which makes me hope the Lord is the nearer.   The Gentiles are rejecting the Gospel, according to Scripture.   Then the Jews shall be gathered in, according to Scripture.   ' Oh, let my lamp be burning when Jesus comes,' is my prayer."

It was this sort of contagious joy which he carried into his work that so fitted him for the "work of an evangelist." He went through the land as one " bearing tidings of great joy."   A pastor writes of him : " He was well named

'*Bliss.*' What a happy man he was! What a ray of sunshine, what a spring of joy in the household! My children will never forget him; and will always think of him as an illustration of the blessed peace and radiant cheerfulness of a Christian life."

Yet he was not one-sided. The Saviour gave him His own joy, and His tenderness also. He knew how Satan was striving with human hearts, and all his solicitude was that men should believe that an Almighty Helper had come to the aid of tempted and fallen humanity. From the hour when Christ called him to pursue these evangelistic labours we find continuous records of his tender and successful services in different parts of the States. He witnessed those conversions which are the breaking of a wonderful love over dreary hearts, but he spoke only of what Christ had wrought by him. There was no fussiness about him— no stepping into the place of pastors. But ministers bear record how audiences were moved under his tones, as the bending grain before the wind; how his voice now thrilled with pitying love, and now exulted in triumphant tones, as he exalted Christ; how hundreds saw through his interpretation of holy words a glory they had not seen in the Saviour; and how churches were raised to a more confident trust. He gave himself wholly to Christ, and the Spirit used him for the glory of the Redeemer.

On March 31, 1874, he writes :—

"My dear wife is fully my equal as a performer, and far superior in matters of taste, criticism, etc. You mistake when you suppose criticism 'hurts' me. I do not want to know the favourable things said about me nearly so much as I desire to hear objections.

"Since writing you before, the way has been very clearly made known to me and my wife for my immediate future.

We have long prayed God to lead me into the widest field of efficient labour.   He has repeatedly come near to us in His delightful, *conscious*, manifestations, and now I am fully persuaded He calls me to give my time and energies to writing and singing the 'Good News.'   I am constrained, by what Christ is and has been to me, to offer all my powers directly to His sweet service.   Beginning with this desire, prompted, I am sure, by the Holy Ghost, I am willing—*we* are willing—to leave ourselves where we always have been, in our Father's loving hands.   He has led us in spite of our plans into all, and only, pleasant and prosperous ways.   It is no time to distrust or question now.   Pardon me if this all sounds like 'cant' to you.   My meaning is to be honest and real.   Pray for us, if you can, that I may be honoured by 'helping Jesus.'   Major Whittle goes with me to preach the gospel while I try to sing it.   Our only aim, sincerely, above all else, is to win souls to Jesus Christ.—Yours in His love,
                                    "P. P. B."

A month or two after he says further of Mrs. Bliss :—

" My wife is in excellent health and spirits, as usual. As she is not to read this, I must say she is an extraordinary woman.   You do not know many women of such unselfish devotion, sublime faith, and child-like trust.   She lives so near the Lord, that I ought to be a good man.   Humanly speaking, my life would have been a failure without her."

Later in the year, we find him in Detroit, where he wrote to his nephew, who was studying medicine, the following characteristic letters :—

                          " Detroit, *October* 9, 1874.
" Dear Will,—Don't you begin to believe that I do not think of you every day.   I believe in you, and in the power

of prayer and a life of faith. You must succeed; and in order to true success, if you would enter into the kingdom of heaven, or of science, or greatness, you must become as a little child, humble and teachable, desirous of being led. I trust you have this spirit in a good degree; keep it. Pray for more faith and trust. Do not apply yourself too closely to books as such. Make haste slowly. Save time by wait- ing for some things. Save health. Confide everything to your loving aunt. She is a faithful friend, though her cor- rections may seem grievous.

"The Meetings are immense; crowds and crowds, many standing all through. And many had to go away from the door of one of the largest churches last evening. Your prayers are being answered. Praise God for it. To Him be *all*, ALL the glory. Amen."

"DETROIT, *November* 17, 1874.

"DEAR W. H. J.,—You are in my thought and prayers daily. I am anxious that your sojourn in Chicago shall do all for you, in every way, that we hope or God intends. I need not say to you, and yet it is a pleasure, your aunt and I are 'glad you came.' Of course I am away so much. *The* important thing to me is that you make it pleasant for her. *She* says you do *that*, so I am content. Thank God. Only do not let the mental do injustice to your physical and spiritual energies. A *holy* man means a *whole* man—sym- metrical, well-balanced; so have a look, my dear boy, each day, into all things concerning the 'full man.' Confide all to Him 'who careth for you.' Pray for much. Be courteous to all, familiar with few, intimate with none.

"The Meetings go on grandly; many souls daily profess Christ, and the church is more and more revived. I have some thrilling incidents to relate when I come home. Pray for the Meeting at Dr. Goodwin's church for Sunday evening

next. Read this little book carefully, and hand it to some
friend. Good-bye.   "Your loving Uncle,
                                        "P. P. B."

In 1875 we find him in Rome, Penn., whence he
writes :—

"DEAR ONES ALL,—I wonder how you all get along so
well as you seem to ; but 'God is great, and God is good.'
We pray for you every day. Received your telegram and
the dear boys' pictures last night ; we are very thankful. The
picture of 'Paul'* is splendid. I think George looks a little
as if he were attending 'clinics,' but am glad for as good a
likeness as this. You may get this after we come home, so
I'll be brief. Expect us on Thursday, if not there before.

"A great and powerful work of grace has begun here.
We all know that God is with us, and souls are being
gathered into the fold. Of all the places in the world
where I should love to work for Christ, this old home of
ours is the most interesting. Oh, how good it is of my
Master to let me tarry here for a few days in His sweet service ! May He abundantly reward you for helping us ! It is
all for His sake. To Him be the glory ! Amen.
                                        "P. P. B."

Again we find him in Louisville, Kentucky, where it is
recorded in a local paper : "The great success, so far as a
religious awakening is concerned, has been something beyond all precedent." He writes of this :—

            "GALT HOUSE, LOUISVILLE, KENTUCKY,
                    "*Feb.* 16, 1875.
"DEAR MOTHER,—I cannot wait—must tell you that the
Lord has done and is doing a great and mighty work here.

---
* His little boy.

Thousands and thousands crowding daily and nightly to hear the old-fashioned gospel of Christ. Three or four Meetings daily; 200 or 250 arose for prayers on Sunday night. This morning I had a glorious praise-meeting in the hotel. Last evening, in the mass meeting in the hall, an immense opera house jammed full—2500 or 3000 people. Among those who arose for prayer, and went down into the inquiry-room with me, and I trust gave her heart to the Lord, was—guess who? My heart is full as I write it— V. . . . D . W. . . . ! Hallelujah! There is joy in heaven!

"If all the Meetings had been carried on, and only this one result, how richly paid I would have been. Yet hundreds of souls just as precious have been saved, we believe. Oh, how good God has been! And how precious Jesus, my Master, is to-day! I write in V.'s name, who sends her love to you all, and asks that you and I set apart Sunday, Feb. 28, to pray for her, and to praise the Lord for His goodness.

"Of course you will pray and praise for me. It is in answer to your prayers of years ago, and to the prayers of him who now dwells in the glory-land, that God has chosen me. Not a day, hardly a Meeting passes, but I think—And can it be, that He has chosen me to be an instrument, a vessel in which to carry the water of life to perishing souls? Oh, pray daily that I may be a vessel sanctified and meet for the Master's use!"

There are those who are doubtful respecting these sudden conversions. Some who object are devout men. But let this be remembered: there are in all congregations persons who are serious but cannot be brought to a decisive choice for Christ. They act best under emotion. They need the impulse of special appeal, and vivid representations

of truth. This is often used to deliver them from the
vacillations or apathy into which they have come. The
powerful apprehension of neglected truths brings them
right over to the side of Christ. If, moreover, the sub-
sequent lives of professed converts were traced, it would
most likely be found that the number of those who have,
after this instantaneous conversion, lived consistent and
devoted lives, has been as large as has been the number of
consistent professors after a more gradual process of change.
There are many who have carefully watched the history of
churches who will confirm this view.

It was the advice of a veteran minister to a young pastor, " Pay attention to the young and the aged; they will
reward you." Yes, the aged will reward, who have come to
look on life as a regret. Precious to them is the theme of
the gospel, which tells only of grace. And the young will
reward much more. No mistake is greater than the sweep-
ing assertion that the impressions of youth are evanescent.
They may be followed by a period that looks doubtful,
but the seed of piety will eventually germinate, and prove
its vitality. Mr. Bliss, like all true workers in the kingdom of Christ, well remembered the importance the Incarnate One attached to childhood. His heart went
forth to the children. He had a remarkable way of interesting them in the Bible, which was the end to which all
his labours tended. It was, however, abhorrent to him to
make religious services a mere entertainment to the young.
He carefully made their interest a means to an end. He
also prepared for Meetings with children. He desired that
their faith should spring up in feeling, and then be directed
by intelligence. He sought in 'Services for the Young' that
his own soul should first of all be gladdened by his love to
the Redeemer; and that love shone through his looks, and
vibrated in tones of song: thus children, who are fine dis-

criminators of the real in character, were attracted to him. His geniality, tenderness, and sympathy, swayed them. Hundreds of children were, it is said, led by him to trust in Jesus as their Helper and Saviour.

Sometimes his illustrations were quaint as he spoke to children ; but his manly bearing and dignified manner preserved him from all approach to the grotesque, which was offensive to him. A little incident which occurred in Peoria will illustrate this. It was just before Christmas, and Mr. and Mrs. Bliss were busy each day in procuring presents to take home to their own little Paul and George. One day, in the street, he noticed, as he was passing, a little girl, poorly clad, standing in front of a toy-store window, gazing intently and longingly at the dolls displayed in large numbers, and in a pretty arrangement, from large to small, in the window. He stopped at once, and kindly and earnestly said, " Now just pick out the one you want, and you shall have it. I will go in and buy it for you." He would have been delighted to do so—had already done it in his own mind ; but the child looked at him with an expression of distrust and unbelief, and, gathering her shawl over her head, hurried away, not heeding his repeated endeavours to win her confidence. " That is just the way sinners treat Christ," said he. " I was really grieved that the little one would not let me do for her what I wanted to, and that she distrusted me, when I just wished with all my heart to make her happy. I think I understand a little better how the Lord feels at our unbelief of His precious promises."

" It seems to many of us," says his companion in travel, " that, ' take him for all in all, we ne'er shall look upon his like again.' He was given to us to show how beautiful a nature may become when sanctified by the indwelling Spirit of God." Yes, from his glorified spirit the voice comes to us, " Yet not I, but the grace of God which was with me."

The secret of a sanctified and effective life lies in one brief sentence—"Trustful loyalty to heavenly teaching, the sure precursor of more abundant grace."

We have seen how, as a poor barefooted boy in the wilder regions of Pennsylvania, he mourned for sin and loved Christ: and how God made him a child of His special care : how, when "a country boy" labouring as a farm-servant, he aspired after truth, and gave his hours to the pursuit of wisdom ; and how God opened for him the book of beauty and knowledge, so that his thoughts discoursed sweetness hour by hour : how, when honour and affection grew around him, he walked the more humbly, and guarded his growing strength by dependence ; and how his nature took a higher tone as God began to make him a power of influence among men : how he cultured in that more elevated sphere the things which are "lovely and of good report," and trained his nature to gentle courtesies ; and how the Spirit of the Father dwelt more richly in his heart, and stamped on his life a grander nobleness : how he then threw heart and soul into that new order of evangelistic movement which, with perfect freedom and unceremonial naturalness, was bringing tempted and sinful men into contact with the Saviour ; and how God helped him to bring forth from the harp of song strains which will go singing of the love of Jesus over all nations, and call forth from all tried and tempted hearts new emotions of trust, hope, and triumph. Surely the difference between man and man lies in the sense of responsibility as to moral and spiritual growth, and the believing perception that God has given to us "*all things* that pertain unto life and godliness." It is not so much by unwearied and vigorous self-discipline that men grow in goodness, as by fidelity to heavenly teaching combined with implicit trust. Thus it is, according to Christ's words, that whosoever uses "that which he hath," receives more abundantly.

Chapter V.

Mr. Bliss as a Composer and Author—His first Sunday-school Hymns —His Habits and Manner of Writing—Incidents that suggested his Hymns—Letter from Mr. Sankey—Last Hymn he Wrote.

THOUSANDS of people who never saw Mr. Bliss feel that they knew and loved him through his Hymns. To them, and to the generation to come, the principal interest in his life will centre around these productions of his pen. It is proposed to collect in this chapter such facts in regard to the composition and use of the best known and most widely used of his songs as will be of interest to the thousands who sing them.

The first song Mr. Bliss wrote, that was used in Sunday-schools or gospel meetings, is the piece entitled, "If Papa were only Ready." He caught the song from reading in a religious paper of a little boy dying and telling his father, just before death came to take him away, that he was afraid "he would not come to heaven because he couldn't leave the store." He wrote the words and music in May, 1867, at Rome, Pennsylvania, and sent it on to Mr. Root, who was much pleased with it, and caused its immediate publication. The following are the words :—

IF PAPA WERE ONLY READY.

I should like to die, said Willie, if my papa could die too,
But he says he isn't ready, 'cause he has so much to do ;
And my little sister Nellie says that I must surely die,
And that she and mamma—then she stopped, because it made me cry.

But she told me, I remember, once while sitting on her knee,
That the angels never weary watching over her and me ;
And that if we're good (and mamma told me just the same before),
They will let us into heaven when they see us at the door.

There I know I shall be happy, and will always want to stay ;
I shall love to hear the singing, I shall love the endless day ;
I shall love to look at Jesus ; I shall love Him more and more
And I'll gather water-lilies for the angel at the door.

There will be none but the holy—I shall know no more of sin ;
There I'll see mamma and Nellie, for I know he'll let them in ;
But I'll have to tell the angel, when I meet him at the door,
That he must excuse my papa, 'cause he couldn't leave the store.

Nellie says, that may-be I shall very soon be called away ;
If papa were only ready, I should like to go to-day ;
But if I should go before him to that world of light and joy,
Then I guess he'd want to come to heaven to see his little boy.

He wrote SEVEN BOOKS of Songs, and many others in a sheet form, besides miscellaneous contributions to musical journals. There was amazing industry, no doubt ; but song-writing was a spontaneous outflow of the emotions and melody with which his soul was filled. When he found that his verses were being used of God to bring out some precious truth of the gospel of love, or some exalting view of Christ his Lord, there was a joy like an angel must find in being sent on some mission of benevolence. He would come to his wife or friend with the theme of a hymn, with his face shining, and his eyes moist with tears, and would ask for prayers that God would bless the song.

He was a very systematic and orderly man in all his surroundings, scrupulously neat in person and apparel; with the sensitiveness of a woman in matters of taste, and a shrinking from all suggestion of vulgarity in anything in him or around him. His study or place of work, where-ever he might be, partook of the nature of the man. His books and papers were in order, and his work prose-cuted in a business-like manner. It pained him to have things in a "helter skelter" way about him. A mis-spelt word in a letter, or the wrong pronunciation of a word in an Address, was to him like a note out of harmony in music. His penmanship was very neat, and his letters and manu-scripts, as completed by him, are without blots or erasures. He never liked to write a letter with a pencil, and would always re-copy a piece of music, if possible, rather than send it to his publishers with erasures. He was, however, so easy and natural in manner, and so free from all self-con-sciousness, that his friends never received an impression of any peculiarity of precision. He did not so much school himself to carry out the system of his own life, and to reach his own lofty ideal, as that his experience was the ful-filment of the Lord's words—" He that abideth in Me, and I in him, the same bringeth forth much fruit." He had, moreover, such a happy and good-humoured way of bearing himself towards the defects he might observe, and such inexpressible tenderness for the feelings of others, as never to produce a shade of uncomfortableness among those who were brought into contact with him.

It was after his consecration to Christ for His service in saving souls, that Mr. Bliss rose to a more habitual apprehen-sion of the personal Saviour. Christ risen—Christ ever pre-sent with us—Jesus, the real, living, personal Jesus of the Gos-pels—came closer and closer to him. His communion with Christ was uninterrupted. Christ was a constant Presence, a

Great Companion; and his songs in these days abounded with
Christ. The last year of his life nearly all the songs he
wrote contain the three themes of Gospel testimony—Christ
died for our sins; He lives for our justification; He is coming
again in a glory which we are to share. He did not plan
these hymns with any purpose to teach these truths, and was
surprised himself when his attention was called to the fact
of the uniformity of their testimony in these directions. He
simply wrote of what filled his own heart and had come to
his own soul. "The Half was never Told," "No other
Name is Given," "Hallelujah! what a Saviour," "Are your
Windows open toward Jerusalem?" "Hallelujah! He is
Risen," "At the Feet of Jesus," "Hallelujah! 'tis Done,"
are examples of the truth of this statement. The words he
used to sing so magnificently filled his soul—

> Christ Jesus is my all in all,
> My comfort, and my love,
> My life below; and He shall be
> My joy and crown above.

And in singing these themes his friends never saw anything
approaching a desire to win admiration. He sang as the lark
mounts to heaven, pouring out his carol as he soars.

It is not claimed in all this that Mr. Bliss was what is
termed "a great poet." Singular to say his modesty was
such that he never classed himself in the list of poets. But
he had a true poetic faculty and feeling, and his culture and
taste were so maturing that had he not been cut off at thirty-
eight he would probably have written hymns which would
have ranked with the finest in the world. As it was, he wrote
hymns adapted to the culture of ordinary persons; and He
who uses things which the world despises uses words which
do not conceal by human wisdom the grand simplicity of
His message of grace to men.

But it was the combination of the musician and the poet

that made Mr. Bliss's character so unique. Who can listen to the sweet solemn strains of "Eternity" in the "LATER SONGS AND SOLOS," to Mrs. Ellen Gates's words, "Oh, the Clanging Bells of Time!"—or to the music which he set to Miss Lathbury's "Arise and Shine!"—without emotion, and a strong impression of the inspiration of the music as a living interpretation of these two impressive hymns? Mr. Root says, "'When Jesus comes' deserves by its music to lie by the side of the best songs of the church; its intellectual side is well enough; its emotional element is to me irresistible; and I venture to say it will live if that deeper consideration to the things of the heart which marks this epoch continues to distinguish religious progress, as I believe it will."

Some of the incidents which suggested the music and words of Mr. Bliss's hymns will interest those who use them.*

His "Whosoever will may Come" was suggested after hearing Mr. H. Moorhouse, of England, preach from the text of all texts—John iii. 16.

On the morning when he wrote "Jesus loves Me," Mrs. Bliss came into the breakfast-room at Chicago, saying that her husband had been singing over a tune which she thought God had given him, and which she had been singing to herself all the morning. The idea her husband wished to teach was that the peace of a Christian is founded on Christ's love to sinful mortals, and not on their love to Him. Ah, what an important distinction is this. No wonder that hundreds of persons bewildered by the teaching which sends them to their own hearts to find evidences of salvation, should be everywhere blessing Mr. Bliss for that hymn. It

---

* A large number of Mr. Bliss's Pieces, Words and Music, will be found in "SACRED SONGS AND SOLOS," and "LATER SONGS AND SOLOS."

is said that in certain cities of Great Britain Mr. Sankey's singing of the hymn produced profound emotion under the surprise of this new view of the unmerited grace of Christ's love.

"Only an Armour - Bearer" was suggested by the beautiful narrative in 1 Sam. xiv.

The exquisite hymn which he himself loved so well, " I know not the Hour when my Lord will come," was suggested to him in reading the book of Miss Phelps, " Gates Ajar," and the criticisms upon it.   Mr. James McGranahan, the composer, was stopping with him ; and after working at a tune for it before the piano during the night, the music came to Mr. McGranahan as an inspiration after waking from a doze in the parlour.   Mr. Bliss immediately adopted it, and the words and music will not soon die.

The following was the suggestion which led to his writing " Pull for the Shore " :

"We watched the wreck with great anxiety. The life-boat had been out some hours, but could not reach the vessel through the great breakers that raged and foamed on the sand-bank. The boat appeared to be leaving the crew to perish.   But in a few minutes the captain and sixteen sailors were taken off, and the vessel went down.

"'When the life-boat came to you, did you expect it had brought some tools to repair your old ship?' I said.

"'Oh no, she was a total wreck. Two of her masts were gone, and if we had stayed mending her only a few minutes, we must have gone down, sir.'

"'When once off the old wreck and safe in the life-boat, what remained for you to do ?'

"'Nothing, sir, but just to pull for the shore.'"

"Down Life's dark Vale we Wander" was written in Peoria, Illinois, in 1872. It was suggested by a conversation with Mrs. Wm. Reynolds and Mrs. Tyng upon the subject of our Lord's personal return. One of the ladies quoted a sentence from a work of Anna Shipton's as to the joy and comfort it gave her, day by day, to think each morning at sunrise, "This may be the day of His coming." Mr. Bliss was much impressed—more deeply so than ever before—by the reality of the subject; and a few days after, as he was coming downstairs from his room with the thought of "looking" for the Lord upon his mind, he commenced singing "Down life's dark vale we wander," the words coming to him as easily as the steps he took down the stairs. He at once wrote it out with the music as now sung.

"Let the Lower Lights be Burning" was written after hearing the following from Mr. Moody :

"On a dark, stormy night, when the waves rolled like mountains and not a star was to be seen, a boat, rocking and plunging, neared the Cleveland harbour.

"'Are you sure this is Cleveland?' asked the captain, seeing only one light from the light-house.

"'Quite sure, sir,' replied the pilot.

"'Where are the lower lights?'

"'Gone out, sir.'

"'Can you make the harbour?'

"'We *must*, or perish, sir!'

"And with a strong hand and a brave heart, the old pilot turned the wheel. But, alas! in the darkness he missed the channel, and with a crash upon the rocks the boat was shivered, and many a life lost in a watery grave. Brethren, the Master will take care of the great light-house: *let us keep the lower lights burning!*"

The Rev. Mr. Brundage tells of the origin of "Almost Persuaded." The closing words of a sermon preached by him were, "He who is almost persuaded is almost saved, but to be almost saved is to be entirely lost." Mr. Bliss being in the audience, was impressed with the thought, and

immediately set about the composition of what proved one
of his most popular hymns, and which Mr. Sankey sang
with such impressiveness on one occasion in the Opera
House, Haymarket.

"More to Follow" was written after hearing Mr. Moody
say :

"A fortune was left in the hands of a minister for
one of his poor parishioners. Fearing that it might be
squandered if suddenly bestowed upon him, the wise minister
sent him a little at a time, with a note saying, '*This is thine;
use it wisely; there is more to follow.*' Brethren, that is just
the way God deals with us."

The popular hymn, "Hold the Fort," has been already
referred to in a quotation from Mr. Root's letter. The
entire story is now given.

"During October, 1864, while the American war of eman-
cipation was proceeding, General Sherman began his famous
march to the sea. While his army lay camped in the neighbourhood of Atlanta, the army of Hood in a carefully-prepared
movement passed the right flank of Sherman's army, and gaining
his rear, commenced the destruction of the railroad leading
north, burning block-houses and capturing the small garrisons
along the line. Sherman's army was put in rapid motion,
following Hood, to save the supplies and larger posts, the principal of which was at Altoona Pass, a defile in the Altoona range
of mountains, through which ran the railroad. General Corse,
of Illinois, was stationed here with a brigade of troops, composed of Minnesota and Illinois regiments—in all, about 1500
men; Colonel Tourtelotte being second in command. A
million and a half of rations were stored here, and it was highly
important that the earthworks commanding the Pass and pro-
tecting the supplies should be held. Six thousand men, under
command of General French, were detailed by Hood to take
the position. The works were completely surrounded and sum-
moned to surrender. Corse refused, and sharp fighting com-

menced. The defenders were slowly driven into a small fort
upon the crest of the hill. Many had fallen, and the result
seemed to render a prolongation of the fight hopeless. At this
moment, an officer caught sight of a white signal flag, far away
across the valley, twenty miles distant, upon the top of Kenesaw
Mountain. The signal was answered, and soon the message
was waved across from mountain to mountain :

"'Hold the Fort ; I am coming.—W. T. SHERMAN.'

"Cheers went up ; every man was nerved to the full appreciation of the position ; and, under a murderous fire, which
killed or wounded more than half the men in the fort—Corse
himself being shot three times, Colonel Tourtelotte taking
command, though also badly wounded—they held the fort for
three hours, until the advance-guard of Sherman's army came
up. French was obliged to retreat."

No incident of the war illustrates more thrillingly the
inspiration imparted by the knowledge of the presence of
the Christian's Commander; that He is cognizant of our
position ; and that, doing our utmost, He will supplement
our weakness by speedy reinforcements. The message of
Sherman to the soldiers of Altoona thus becomes the
message of the Great "Captain of our salvation," who
signals ever to all who fight life's battle,—"Hold the Fort."

It was in May, 1870, that Mr. Bliss on hearing of this
fact in Rockford, Illinois, wrote the hymn and music beginning with the stirring words, "Ho! my comrades, see
the signal."

Just before Christmas, 1871, Mrs. Bliss asked a friend,
"What shall I get for my husband as a Christmas present?"
and, at the suggestion of this friend, purchased and presented him with the bound volume of a monthly English
periodical called "Things New and Old." Many things in
these books of interpretation of Scripture and illustrations
of Gospel truth were blessed to him, and from the reading
of something in one of these books, in connection with

Romans viii. and Hebrews x. 10, was suggested this glorious Gospel song: " Once for All."

In compiling GOSPEL SONGS, in 1874, Mr. Bliss desired to publish in it the well-known hymn, " Hallelujah, Thine the Glory," then much used in religious services. The owners of the copyright of the hymn declined his application for its use, and he wrote " Hallelujah ! 'tis Done," to supply the want. Many have been led to decide for Christ by this hymn, and the church has reason to rejoice at that refusal.

" Hallelujah ! He is Risen ! " was written with the music in 1876, and on an Easter afternoon was first sung to an audience of five thousand people in the Court House Square, Augusta, Georgia. " None present," it is recorded, " will ever forget the radiant face, and the triumphant ringing tones with which he sang it."

" The Holy Spirit : Resist not, Grieve not, Quench not," was suggested to him by B. F. Jacobs. He loved the song himself, and the words are among the most beautiful he has written. He felt that more should be sung of the Holy Spirit and His work, and therefore wrote this.

" Wishing, Hoping, Knowing," he wrote to bring into a more full assurance of salvation those Christians whom he met with in Gospel meetings, and who were looking to their feelings for peace instead of to the living Christ.

" Will You Meet Me at the Fountain ? " was suggested by the cursory use of these words by a friend at the Chicago Exposition, in 1873, as they parted to make the inspection of the building. The remark awoke in his heart the suggestion of another meeting, and blossomed out into the beautiful song.

" Seeking to Save " was suggested by a conversation of Mr. Bliss, with Dr. Wadsworth, of the Methodist Episcopal Church of Mobile, Alabama, upon the unity of the three parables in the fifteenth chapter of Luke.

The following letter from his friend and co-worker, Mr. Sankey, will be read with peculiar interest at this time :—

"It was in the autumn of 1870 that I for the first time met P. P. Bliss. I had just arrived in Chicago to join Mr. Moody in his work in that city, and had gone with him to attend the noon-day prayer meeting in Lower Farwell Hall. Mr. Bliss was leading the singing, and at the close of the meeting Mr. Moody demanded of us a song. Seating himself at the piano which was in the room, we sang from 'Hallowed Songs : '—

> " ' Oh, think of the Home over there,
>   By the side of the River of Light,
> Where the saints, all immortal and fair,
>   Are robed in their garments of white,
>   Over there, over there.'

"This was our first song together ; and the last one we sang a few days before he passed 'Over There,' was 'Hallelujah ! what a Saviour !' It was my pleasure to have met Mr. Bliss very often afterward, in the Saturday noon meetings for the study of the International Sunday School Lessons. In these meetings, as well as in the usual daily prayer meetings, he was always a blessing and an inspiration.

"During the time I was in Chicago, prior to our going to England, I became familiar with many of Mr. Bliss's songs, and they struck me as being specially adapted for reaching the masses ; and, that I might have them in convenient shape for use in evangelistic work, I gathered a number of them from his 'Charm' and 'Sunshine,' and with other sacred songs, arranged them into a 'Musical Scrap Book,' which, with my Bible, was the only book I took with me across the sea.

"It was while singing from this scrap book, 'Jesus of Nazareth Passeth By,' 'Prodigal Child, Come Home,' and

Mr. Bliss's ' Hold the Fort,' ' Jesus Loves Me,' and ' Free
from the Law,' in the old cathedral city of York, and in
Sunderland, England, that we began fully to realize the
wonderful power there was in these Gospel songs.   The
demand for them soon became so great that we were compelled to have them published in a cheap form, which we
did, under the title of ' SACRED SONGS AND SOLOS.'   This
collection contained a number of Mr. Bliss's best songs,
which, together with a companion book of ' Words Only '
(the latter being sold for a penny), is believed to have
attained a larger circulation than any collection of Hymns
and Tunes ever published.

"The first of Mr. Bliss's hymns that became popular in
Great Britain was ' Jesus Loves Even Me,' and, more than
any other hymn, it became the key-note of our meetings
there.   The next song which became immensely popular
was ' Hold the Fort,' and it is to-day, perhaps, the most
popular sacred song in England or America.

"I should think Mr. Bliss's ' Almost Persuaded ' has
won more souls to the Saviour than any other hymn written
by him.

"It has been no unusual thing, in our Special Meetings
for young converts, to have them testify that it was the
singing of ' Almost Persuaded,' or ' What shall the Harvest
be?' that led them to decide for Christ.   During the last
year, ' Waiting and Watching' has been specially blessed,
and we believe that through the singing of this little hymn,
thousands have been led to desire to live a better and
a holier life.   This song, with many of his new ones, will
ever have a deeper and a tenderer meaning to us, now that
he has entered within the gates into the city of the great
King, where he may be ' waiting and watching' for us.   And
with what new joy and rejoicing shall we now sing his sweet
words !—

" ' Many loved ones have I in yon heavenly throng ;
They are safe now in glory, and this is their song :
Hallelujah ! 'tis done ! I believe on the Son,
I am saved by the blood of the Crucified One.'

" ' He was not, for God took him.' (Gen. v. 24.)

[signature: Ira D. Sankey]

" BOSTON, *February*, 1877."

———

" The last words," writes Major Whittle, " that I know of
his writing were the two pieces, ' My Redeemer,' and ' I've
Passed the Cross of Calvary.' Nothing that he ever wrote
made him more happy. I can see him now, as he came
into my room at Peoria and stood by my table, with the
words of the latter piece written in pencil, and I can hear
his earnest voice as he read the verses and called my attention to the ' Empty tomb ' and the ' 'Vantage ground.' The
tears filled his eyes as he stood for a moment and spoke of
the risen Christ, the acceptance we have in Him, and the
victory over sin and over the flesh that faith in this acceptance gives to the believer. ' Now,' he said, ' if the Lord
will give me a tune for this, I believe it will be used to bring
some souls on to the mountain.' The Lord gave him a tune
during the last week of his life at Rome, Penn. He sang
it to the family with inspiring effect, but the written music
then used was burned at Ashtabula. It was one of a few
pieces that he placed in his satchel, to look over during his
journey. The family are all musicians, but cannot recall
the melody that inspired them that evening, and we shall
not hear it as he sang it until we stand with him in the

resurrection morning so rapidly hastening on, and know, with him, the fulness of Christ's resurrection power.   I think that then, among the voices of the redeemed, we shall distinguish his, and hush our praises for a moment to listen to the tune the Lord had given him as he sings—

> " ' Oh, glorious height of 'vantage ground !
>   Oh, blest victorious hour ! '

"God grant, to all who read, a part in that first resurrection."

Such testimony on the part of his faithful colleague in evangelistic services may seem partial.   But letters from others who remain speak of "the golden days which were spent with him," and of "the graceful halo" that hung over him.   Those who shared in these re-unions testify also of "the glowing happiness" which he diffused on summer days when he would unite with his friends "amid the twining branches of a neighbouring grove" in singing little quartettes. It was his grace and gladness of heart through abiding union with Christ which deepen the preciousness of his memory to those who knew him.   Oh, what would it be if this "joy of the Lord" came into the hearts of all of us who have believed on the Lord !   How would the Church be multiplied, and "the tabernacle of God" appear to have come down among men !

Chapter VI.

The Work of an Evangelist—Gospel Meetings—Visit to Kenesaw Mountain—At Chicago—At Home—Philadelphia Exhibition—Night Scene—Dr. Vincent's Tribute.

T will have been observed that ministers of the gospel invited Mr. Bliss and his companion in the service of Christ to visit their churches. There was no jealousy on their side, and no assumption on his. And this fact will explain the value of his work. When we read of large numbers brought to decide for Christ, let it be remembered that to pastors who "watch for souls," there are no persons who awaken a more distressing interest than those who sit year after year beneath the sound of the truth, and remain apparently only on the borders of the kingdom of Christ. They are not openly of the world ; they respect and even love their pastors ; they are among the most regular in the Sabbath services of God's house. But they never "confess with the mouth the Lord Jesus," and there is a painful doubt as to their spiritual safety. To bring such persons right over to Christ is to bring an untold satisfaction and even gladness into their life. None can be more anxious than godly ministers for something that shall break the monotony of service that lulls such persons into an unbroken apathy. If, then, the voice of the minister has become a familiar sound, let the unprofessional voice of the layman be heard. If preaching Christ does not win, let some one come to "teach and admonish in psalms and hymns and spiritual songs." "There are diversities of gifts, but the same Spirit; and there are differences of administrations, but the same Lord." Only let it be observed it is no evidence that there is no genuine work of conversion because repentance has not been the prominent feature. The marked and prominent feature of the entire conversion of those "not far from the kingdom of God" will be their realization of the *grace* of the gospel, and their closing with Christ as the Saviour of men.

Among the testimonies to Mr. Bliss's peculiar work must be reckoned those of ministers of the Gospel of all denominations. Dr. R. F. SEMPLE, of Minneapolis, records :—

"I had come to know him intimately, to love him tenderly, and to confide in him implicitly. There certainly have been few men so loving, unselfish, and kind. He was singularly artless. He wore no disguise. In presence dignified and commanding, as Saul among the children of Israel, he was in spirit simple, and unostentatious, and confiding as a child. His songs were like himself. They were the utterances of his own great heart. They claimed no relation, and had none, to the measured and lofty poetry of the Homeric hymns. They were sweet lyrics rather. The most intellectual were moved by them. The unlearned understood them. They were fragrant with the love of Jesus, and I doubt not led many to Him. Though born within the last decade, they have overtaken the sacred hymns of Watts, and Newton, and Toplady; and some of them will live as long.

"This dear brother has sown seeds in the hearts of many whom I know, which I fervently hope shall yet bring forth immortal fruitage in their salvation. How tenderly did he speak to the young of Christ, the children's Friend, and urge them to come to Him! How earnestly did he pray that they might know Jesus, and rejoice in His light. The memory of those days will abide with us down to the winter of life, and we shall always be thankful that our dear brethren in Christ, Whittle and Bliss, came this way; loving evangelists, who pointed us to the wicket gate of Mercy, and bade us hasten to it.

*　　*　　*　　*　　*

" I recall a sweet and solemn evening, when our dear brother and his equally lovely wife sang together a hymn which was prophetic of their end—may it be of our peaceful departure :

> " ' Through the valley of the shadow I must go,
> Where the cold waves of Jordan roll ;
> But the promise of my Shepherd will, I know,
> Be the rod and staff of my soul.' "

The Rev. G. C. WATERMAN writes :—

" Philip Bliss was my friend. I loved him as a brother, and have good reason to believe that the love was returned in full measure. My acquaintance with him began a few years before he went to Chicago, and up to that time was intimate, so that a friendship struck its roots into our hearts which has lived and grown through ten years of separation. He was a frequent guest at my house, coming sometimes alone, sometimes with Mr. Towner, and sometimes bringing his wife with him, but always welcome. His personal appearance and bearing were such as to attract and win respect and friendship wherever he went. Nature had lavished upon him a profusion of charms. Not Saul nor David was more eminent among his fellows for manly beauty. Homer would have put him high among his heroes and described him with his choicest epithets. He was at once dignified and genial ; a subtle and peculiar grace, which never degenerated into softness or sickly sentimentality, invested all that he did or said. Behind this there lay, not quite concealed, no small amount of power."

At a Conference, held by the pastors of several Evangelical churches of Louisville, Kentucky, representing the Presbyterian, Methodist, Baptist, Episcopal, and Lutheran churches, the Rev. Stuart Robinson presented the following memorial minute, which was unanimously adopted :—

" In view of the peculiar and interesting relations of Christian friendship growing out of the labours of Messrs. Whittle and Bliss as evangelists, so remarkably blessed of God among us, we deem it eminently appropriate that some formal public expression be given of our sense of their labours.

"We desire to bear an affectionate testimony to the signally elevated Christian character of these servants of Christ, so earnest and faithful, yet withal so modest and unassuming, and so wise in winning souls. We recall with gratitude to God the marvellous gifts and culture of the sweet Gospel singer whose strains were blessed of God as the means of comforting and edifying God's people, of encouraging despondent souls, of determining the halting, of directing the inquiring, and of awakening the souls slumbering in sin.*

---

* An objection has been made that the effect in England of Mr. Moody and Mr. Sankey's work, aided by Mr. Bliss's hymns, has been transient. But there are pastors who entirely controvert this statement when it is made too broadly. One proof may be given. In a Church Manual of Highbury Chapel, Birmingham, for the year ending 1876, the Rev. W. F. Callaway states :—" The warm flush of life and energy which came from the work of Mr. Moody has somewhat subsided. But not without having done us permanent good. We are, I am sure, more

The Rev. D. W. MORGAN, of Griggsville, writes in a similar strain, and gives the following incident respecting Mrs. Bliss :—

" Mr. and Mrs. Bliss came, and the first evening, as we were seated about the fire, Mrs. Bliss said, ' Mr. Morgan, I do not think you need to go South for the recovery of your throat, nor even to give up preaching or singing. I think I can tell what is the difficulty with your throat, and can point out its remedy. It is brought on by a vicious elocution. You are using an *assumed* tone of voice, and are probably unconsciously imitating some one's voice that you have admired. The *orotund* is not your natural voice. By its use you have laid an undue stress on the larynx and vocal chords, and they have yielded to over-tension. Your remedy is to adopt, arbitrarily, a more *tenor* key of voice. Raise it at least two tones in conversation, reading, and preaching.' I thanked her, but replied that I thought her remedy altogether impracticable, that I could not take up at once another tone of voice. But she insisted that it could be done, that they would be with us for two weeks, would watch me closely, and help to enforce the cure. I tried it, sang in most sessions of the Convention, and preached the next Sabbath. My throat gained strength, and I have never from that day missed a religious or other service in consequence of disordered throat. The hint may be worth the attention of other public speakers and singers."

---

hopeful, more confident in God's power, and more full of longing for the salvation of men. Of all among us whom I have known as persons who were blessed through Mr. Moody's meetings, not one has turned back. Many who were an anxiety and fear before, are now a comfort and joy. A good number of young people, many of whom owe much to the services (conducted by Mr. Moody) in Bingley Hall, conduct two Ragged Schools in the heart of the town, with resolute courage and perseverance."

Nor was it ministers only who wrote favourably of Mr. Bliss. A gentleman in St. Paul, Minnesota, says :—

"We cannot in St. Paul speak of him as we knew him long ago ; in other communities he grew up, and in other places had his most intimate associations. But he was nevertheless our fellow-citizen, our friend, our brother. In an emphatic and peculiar sense he had no continuing city ; no West, no East, no North, no South could claim him. Wherever souls needed the divine blessing and comfort of the Gospel ; wherever there were those whose sensibilities could be touched by the sweetest of music, the glad evangel of salvation by Christ—there was Bliss's home for the hour, the day, the week, the month. He counted all men as brethren, and his heartfelt desire was that all, like himself, should turn their faces to the heavenly Jerusalem, and, accepting the Saviour, whose love he so sweetly sang, be ready at any moment for the summons which should call them to be its inhabitants.

"At the County Gaol, at the County Hospital, at the State Reform School, he held services, always striving to appear at his best, and give those who heard him at these places the very sweetest of his efforts.

"His modesty about his musical attainments was always apparent, but at no time more so than when in the praise-meeting, which he held while here : though the Opera House was filled by the hope of hearing him sing often, he did not give a single solo piece during the whole two hours of service."

Such was the service of Mr. Bliss in the closing months of his life. God gave him, as He did John the Baptist, to be a witness of the Lamb of God, and then withdrew him from the scene. But the echoes of his voice remain, and especially of his utterances during the year 1876, when his friends thought that he grew very rapidly in grace, and his work rounded out to completion. His own heart, through all these services, found the abiding calm which he expressed in his sweet, little hymn :—

> In Me ye may have peace ;
> My peace I give to you.
> Rest, troubled soul, rest in the Lord,
> His love will bear thee through.
>
> In Me ye may have peace ;
> Though wars against thee rise,
> Hope thou in God, be not dismayed,
> Lift up thy weeping eyes.
>
> In Me ye may have peace ;
> Dear Lord, our refuge be,
> In weal or woe, in life or death,
> We would abide in Thee.

We will sketch his work through the year 1876, *i.e.*, so far as we can. His work in the closet who can sketch ? It is the prayer, which gives all the glory to God, that originates effects. " That men may see and consider and understand together that the hand of the Lord hath done this, and that the Holy One of Israel hath created it" (Isa. xli. 20). In January he was in Wisconsin ; at Racine and Madison Christians were blessed, and undecided ones led to Christ. In the latter place Mr. Bright, the pastor of the Baptist Church, who was much attached to him, died suddenly in the pulpit, and Mr. Bliss spoke powerfully on the event, and expressed a wish for such a departure. In St. Louis, later in the month, we find him labouring in a Presbyterian pulpit. In that city he remained until March, young people being specially helped by his visit. Among the prisoners in the City Gaol, and in Reformatory Institutions, his voice reached the hearts and touched the consciences of many who had been hopeless ones.

He himself writes to his nephew of the work in St. Louis :—

"'Three to five thousand souls every day, fifty to one hundred asking prayers daily, and individual souls hungry for conversation privately, *personally*, is the condition of things from my standpoint. Our prayers and expectations are that this last week will be the best of all. Pray for us daily.

" I have been to the Missouri Medical College, where the boys at first made fun, extemporized burlesque 'Whittle and Bliss' meetings, sang Gospel songs, etc. Now they are decidedly serious. All come to the Rink.* Some happy young converts. One said if we would continue another week, he believed the whole college would be converted. They have earnest, bold, Christian professors. I also had the opportunity of reaching one hundred and fifty young ladies in a seminary with good results."

In March he went to Mobile, Alabama, to fill an appointment for a Gospel meeting. The route chosen was by rail to Vicksburg, Mississippi, thence by steamer to New Orleans, and on to Mobile by rail. Mrs. Bliss accompanied him, and the trip was a great source of pleasure to them both. In the evening, upon the steamboat, Mr. Bliss entertained the passengers for half-an-hour or more in singing at the piano ; and at the close, when the captain, and all who could come into the cabin, were collected, he would sing a familiar hymn, and then very pleasantly propose and lead in worship. The visit to Mobile was a delightful one. The pastors, the mayor (an excellent Christian man), and Christian people generally, manifested the utmost cordiality and kindness, and did all

---

* Where the Meetings were held.

in their power to make the meetings a success. God was pleased to add His blessing upon the efforts put forth, and many were impressed by Gospel truth, and persuaded to confess Christ. Mr. Bliss's meetings for young people, held in the Baptist church, were much blessed. The church was crowded each afternoon, and very many were led to the Saviour by his preaching of Christ in song, his glowing Bible instruction, and tender personal appeal.

Never did his singing seem more effective than in one of the meetings held in this city, on Sunday evening, in the Opera House. The audience was composed entirely of men, and crowded every part of the house. A solemnity came over all who listened to his deep, sweet voice, and there was hardly a dry eye in the audience. Nearly two hundred men sought an interest in the prayers of Christians that night.

After ten days in Mobile, Mr. Bliss went to Montgomery, and conducted services in the City Hall. Great interest was at once manifested, and the meetings were largely attended. The pastors and people, as at Mobile, were most hospitable and cordial in the welcome extended to their Northern brethren. Here, as in Mobile, special pains were taken to hold services for the coloured people, and arrangements made for their attending the general meetings. Mr. Bliss's singing was greatly enjoyed by them, and he in turn was much moved by their wild and plaintive melodies. After his song, " Father, I'm tired," they broke down in uncontrollable emotion. His labours at Montgomery closed in a meeting participated in by all the pastors, and where not a few confessed to a hope in Christ.

From Montgomery Mr. Bliss went to Selma, and here again conducted young people's meetings, with precious fruit for Christ. From Selma Mrs. Bliss returned to Chicago to arrange for closing up their house for a summer's removal to Rome, Penn., leaving Mr. Bliss to fill an appoint-

ment at Augusta, Georgia. The trip to Augusta was made
viâ the Selma and Dalton Railroad through Georgia, and
thence to Atlanta, to give Mr. Bliss an opportunity to
visit Kenesaw Mountain, where occurred the incident that
gave rise to the song, "Hold the Fort." He remained
in Augusta only five days, but was much used of God
during that time. On Easter Sunday he sang in the
open air, at a Meeting held in the Court-house square.
Between three and four thousand people were present, and
gave the most rapt attention as he sang " Hallelujah, He is
Risen," and other Gospel songs. His afternoon service was
crowded with people, and much religious interest immediately developed. His earnest words there of testimony
for the Lord will not soon be forgotten.

On April 17th, Mr. Bliss left Augusta for Chicago. Here
he packed away his books and papers, intending to return
at the close of the year. Alas! unknown to him it was a
final disposition of his earthly effects. On May 1st, accompanied by his wife and two children, he started for the old
home in Pennsylvania. His affectionate nature craved
family love, and he felt he needed the summer rest for new
literary work, and for renewing the springs of thought at the
heavenly fountains. How those prayers were ripening his
spirit for the translation that awaited him, only the heavenly
watchers know. Pleasant to him was that summer of 1876.
Familiar scenes delighted him. Friends came in troops
about him. He "took to" people; never carped nor
criticised. He was, says one, during that summer, simple
as a child, ever bearing himself as a man of God, but without a touch of asceticism, and with all the freshness of
youth. He enjoyed the society of his fellow-men, and his
intercourse overflowed with geniality.

During the summer he visited the Philadelphia Exhibition, passed a week at the home of Mr. Moody, at North-

field, Mass., and went to the Christian Assembly at Chautauqua. Dr. J. H. Vincent, conductor of the Assembly, thus writes concerning him at that time :—

"Mr. Bliss was one of the noblest and one of the gentlest of men. He had the delicacy of a woman and the strength of a man. His physique was magnificent. I think he was one of the most handsome men I ever met. Large, well proportioned, graceful, with a fine, manly face, full of expression. That body of his was a grand instrument of music, and from its strength came forth sweetness and power. His voice was deep, of wonderful compass and pathos. As it rang out through the woods at Chautauqua, the most thoughtless would stop and listen. Its marvellous magnetic charm was intensified by the energy of the Divine Spirit, which so thoroughly possessed the body and soul of the sweet singer. To the utmost transparency of his pure and simple character he added a fervent and childlike faith. He was a rare Christian. He knew, and believed, and enjoyed, and lived, and preached, and sang, the Gospel of Christ. I never knew a man more thoroughly imbued with the Christian spirit. He had one aim and one work in life. He was always on the look-out for souls. He coveted, above everything else, spiritual results. At our 'Sunday School Assembly,' in private conversation, in the prayer-meetings, in the eventide conferences, on the platform, everywhere, he seemed absorbed in this one great work. Mrs. Bliss was in every way worthy of the noble companion of her life and death. Like him, she was remarkably pure and simple."

On the occasion of that Assembly at Chautauqua, amid the shades of those summer nights, Mrs. Bliss's rich alto voice was heard with her husband's, pouring forth its volumes of music. The concourse of people was immense,

and as the night darkened and the stars shone as silent
preachers of divine majesty, those who listened bear record
that amidst the hushed stillness, the voices which called
to repentance, and testified that the coming of the Lord
drew near, sounded like strains calling out of the depths of
eternity.

May we say, in closing this chapter, we can but wonder
at the disposition of those, calling themselves Christians,
who can sit entranced with passages from operas of doubtful morals, or even with divine words from sacred oratorios
which fall from the lips of men and women who sell their
professional powers for the entertainment of the public, and
can hear, with a curled lip of scorn, of pure and holy ones
who use their gifts without earthly reward in exalting the
praises of Him who gave His life for the world, and by
pleading words of song seek to instil emotion and trust into
human hearts. Thus Mr. Bliss sang of all who served with him
in the Gospel :—

> Welcome, welcome, welcome,
>   Messengers of love !
> Kindred souls with joy are swelling,
>   Like the blest above.
> Welcome, welcome, welcome,
>   Joy illumes our way ;
> Love shall reign in every bosom
>   With unbounded sway.
>
> Praises, praises, praises,
>   For the sacred past,
> For the mercies, rich, abundant,
>   Freely o'er us cast ;
> Praises, praises, praises,
>   For the glad to-day,
> For the future, grand and glorious
>   Praise, oh, praise for aye !

Chapter VII.

*The Last Earthly Labours—In Chicago with Evangelists—In Michigan
—Impressive Scenes in Farwell Hall, Chicago.*

HE end was drawing on. Like a seraph that had
to preach the Gospel in a brief time, the latter
months of 1876 were filled up by Mr. Bliss in
unceasing labours. In September he accompanied Mr. Moody in a preaching tour, and thus writes :
" Just returned from a week of visitations with Brother
Moody, driving over one hundred miles and holding eleven
meetings in Vermont, Massachusetts, and New Hampshire
hills."

In October we find him in Chicago, the guest of Mr.
H. M. Thomson, of Brevoort House, writing and editing
GOSPEL HYMNS, No. 2,* and present at the opening and
memorable services of Messrs. Moody and Sankey. After
that he spent a fortnight with Mr. Sankey at his hotel.
Hitherto their publishing arrangements had been by correspondence ; now they enjoyed what they had long desired
—a season of personal conference, that cemented more
closely the bonds of brotherhood between them.

The hundreds of those who have compared and criticised these two men, and, judging of what is in us all by

---

* GOSPEL HYMNS, No. 2, is reproduced almost in its entirety in
" LATER SONGS AND SOLOS."

nature, have thought of them as in any manner envious or jealous of one another, would have a clearer apprehension of what the grace of God in the heart can do, if they could have known the loving relationship that existed between them. It was a scene long to be remembered, to be with them alone for an hour in the room at the Pacific Hotel, as they compared and tested and criticised the songs to be used in their Meetings. First, one would be at the organ rendering a song, then the other, and both laughing, crying, and praying together over their work. They rejoiced in each other's gifts, and praised God for the honour conferred upon them in being used in His service.

. To Mr. Bliss fault-finding was always offensive, and he would never listen, if he could avoid it, to depreciation of others. In all the writer's fellowship with him, says Major Whittle, he cannot recall an unkind or envious expression toward those whom he may have esteemed better singers, or of greater reputation than himself. God answered to him in a remarkable degree his prayer that he might be—

> Only an instrument, ready
>   His praises to sound at His will,
> Willing, should He not require me,
>   In silence to wait on Him still.

During his sojourn in Chicago, many precious gatherings of brethren consecrated to evangelistic work were enjoyed by Mr. Bliss. Needham and Stebbins, Moorhouse, Charles Inglis, Rockwell, Morton, Jacobs, Farwell, Spafford, Dean, and others were frequently together in those days, dining with Mr. Moody, and discussing Gospel truths or plans of work, or in Mr. Bliss's room listening to some new song. These brethren and others engaged in the work were all dear to Mr. Bliss, and were many times mentioned by name in his prayers. He delighted to hear of the blessing of God upon their labours, and their growth in grace.

October 21st, the brethren separated for their different posts near Chicago. Mr. Bliss went to Kalamazoo, Michigan, Mrs. Bliss accompanying him. The evening of their arrival, they were entertained at the Rev. Mr. Spencer's, where, with thoughtful hospitality, all the pastors of the city were gathered to give them welcome. It was a very pleasant and profitable meeting, and was often referred to both by Mr. and Mrs. Bliss. The Meetings held here were participated in by all the ministers, and from the first were much blessed. Mr. Bliss conducted a young people's meeting with happy results. He ministered in the young ladies' seminary, and at the Baptist College; and in many private residences he sang to the sick and invalid ones. A dear friend there, who for seven years or more had been confined to his room, will well remember the sunshiny day when Mr. Bliss came and sang to him the "Ninety and Nine," "Hallelujah! what a Saviour!" and how, in the seasons of prayer and reading the Word that followed this visit, he gave his heart to the Lord.

The young man who met Mr. and Mrs. Bliss in the singing room, grown reckless from repeated failures in his "experiments" at becoming a Christian, will never forget the pressure of the hands that were so kindly placed upon his shoulders, or the earnest, loving look from the eyes that met his, or the words so earnestly spoken, telling him that his failure had come from his experiments, and urging him now, without experimenting, to trust Christ fully for all things, and make full commitment of his soul to Him. Very earnestly did both these dear friends pray for this young man; and on the day of their departure they took their leave of him, an intelligent, decided, happy Christian. Never will dear H. forget the interest taken in his conversion by Mr. Bliss, nor the sympathy and faith of Mrs. Bliss when, with his dear parents, they were praying to God for his salvation. H. afterwards received from Mr. Bliss the following :—

"JACKSON, MICH., *November* 20, 1876.

"God bless you, my dear friend H., or 'Brother Fred,' as I prefer to call you. It is just as I expected. Your letter did not surprise me one bit.

"Welcome to the ranks! Now 'Forward! march!' in the service of our Captain. You are not the man to sit still and prosper. And I am so glad, Fred, that you have begun in time to put in a full day's work. So here is my heart's 'Good Cheer!' and I expect to see you take both hands and pull with a will. The kind of Christian you are to be will be largely determined in the next few months—I might have said, weeks.

"Lend a hand to that score or more of your associates and the college boys. Pull them in shore before they drift down to the rapids. Help some weak friend by a lift of his burden.

"Oh, how the world needs happy, singing, joyful young Christians!

"I congratulate you upon the good times you are going to have in the service of the Lord. If the Devil knocks you down occasionally, you will fall on your knees; and then he will soon leave you. Good is the Lord. Amen.

"Should have replied sooner, but hoped to see you. We all go to Chicago to-morrow night. Love to father, mother, and sisters.

"Yours in Galatians ii. 20,

"P. P. BLISS.

"Just beginning to get hold here. Pray for us."

One evening, at Kalamazoo, while on the way to the service, this verse was repeated and became a favourite, being almost daily quoted :—

In peace I go ; no fear I know,
 Since Christ walks by my side ;
His love to me my joy shall be,
 His words shall be my guide.

Among the papers found in his trunk, after the catastrophe, was a slip with this verse written upon it. *" Whatever comes,* let us just stick to that," he would remark, and it
truly expressed the atmosphere in which in those days he
seemed to be walking.

Each day the Master gave him some special work, some
special blessing. Some years before, he had given a concert in Kalamazoo, and was entertained for the night by a
gentleman who died a little time after. Mr. Bliss sought
out the family, and found a representative of them in a
daughter who had married a well-known business man, but
neither of them were Christians. God used his visit to
them, and both were led, before the public Meetings
closed, to accept Christ, and are now among the most active
Christian workers of the place.

Another letter, received from a young lady in Kalamazoo,
tells its own story as to the faithfulness of Mr. and Mrs. Bliss
to *individual* souls—the simple secret of all success in evangelistic work, from the time that Jesus talked with Nicodemus
by night and the woman of Samaria at noon, to the present
hour.

Faithfulness in private work with individuals must keep
pace with service in public to the crowds. This personal
dealing with souls is the deciding power oft-times.

From the 11th to the 21st of November, Mr. Bliss was
in Jackson, Michigan, in Union Meetings. He was much
used here, and was in an unusual degree anxious to talk
personally with the unsaved. The first Sunday evening he
conducted a Meeting of his own in the Rev. Mr. Maile's
church, and with much blessing. A dear friend, employed

by the railroad company, with his wife, was present that evening, and remained for personal conversation with him. They were singers, and were glad to have him talk with them; and before he left them, both accepted Christ. That friend is now leading the singing in the church where he was converted, and is spoken of by the pastor as one of his most active workers.

The Michigan State Prison is located at Jackson, and on the two Sunday mornings of Mr. Bliss's stay in the city, he conducted service for the eight hundred inmates there. The most tender, eloquent, and earnest appeal that could have possibly been made to sinners to accept the love of Christ was made by him at his last Meeting with these prisoners on November 19th. He spoke of their homes, and of the little children who missed their fathers; told them of his own dear little Paul going around the room, kneeling at the different chairs, and praying for his papa and mamma; then turned all their awakened sympathies to Christ, by speaking of how impossible it would be for him to give up his dear little boy to die for others, and to die a death of great suffering, and those for whom he died to be his enemies. "Oh, friends," he said, with tears, "I could not do it, but this is what God did for you. He loved you and gave His Son to die for you." The Spirit of God was upon Mr. Bliss that morning in that prison, and the hearts of those hardened men melted like wax. Defiant faces softened and changed with earnest, tender, sympathetic feeling. The animal and sensuous expression passed away as they looked upon that earnest countenance, and saw the tears falling as he pleaded with them, and then sang so tenderly,—

Man of Sorrows! What a name
For the Son of God, who came
Rebel sinners to reclaim!
Hallelujah! what a Saviour!

Two-thirds of the prisoners seemed quite broken down by the reality of the things of God. They never will forget the service of that hour. A strange realization of the presence of the Saviour came over one who was present at the time, and he testifies to the changed and softened expression upon the faces of the men as they listened to Mr. Bliss's words. It seemed to be an explanation of the words spoken of Christ: "Then drew near unto Him publicans and sinners, for to hear Him." There was something of the Lord's own magnetic sympathy and love upon His dear servant that day.

His personal interest in the unsaved was made manifest by an incident that occurred in Jackson, Georgia. Late one evening he went to the telegraph office in the depôt, to send a message. While writing his dispatch, an operator came in, and, without noticing Mr. Bliss, commenced speaking about the Meeting to the two or three railroad officials who were in the room. The young man objected very strongly to a statement in the sermon, that, no matter how sincere people were in their belief, they were lost if they rejected God's truth. "Well," said Mr. Bliss, " is it not like this? Suppose a man wants to go to Chicago to-night; and he makes a mistake, and when the Detroit train comes from the west, he takes it and goes east. Thinking very sincerely that he is on his way to Chicago will not help him a bit. He must believe what the conductor tells him—that he is wrong, and must face about; or he will never reach Chicago." The railroad men chimed in an assent to this illustration. " Just what happened on my train the other day," said a conductor; "a man was going east, when he wanted to go west, and I had hard work to make him believe he was wrong." It was late and Mr. Bliss was very tired, but for some time he remained speaking to this friend. Nor did he forget the interview. Each day Mr. Bliss prayed for this young man, and the very last person he spoke to in Jackson was this operator, urging him to accept Christ and take his stand as His follower.

The stay in Jackson was a very brief one, but blessed of God to many souls. The closing Meeting, held in the Methodist Church, Mr. Bliss often referred to as one of the best of the year. After the preaching of the Gospel, he sang, " I have a Saviour—He's pleading in glory," with its sweet refrain, " For you I am praying, I'm praying for you."* He sang this piece often, and poured out his heart in real prayer as he sang. While singing it one evening, his heart going out for sinners, he added this verse, not found in the song as usually printed :—

> And Jesus is calling—how can you reject Him ?
> He says He loves sinners, so then He loves you :
> O friend, *do* believe it, *arise* and accept Him,
> Give Jesus your heart, while I'm praying for you.

That night in Jackson, as he sang, a hundred or more arose, and the Spirit of God was felt in power in the Meeting. After his singing, prayer was offered, asking that those impressed might then and there decide and fully accept Christ as their Saviour, as presented to them in the revealed Word of God.

Such was the new and strange gladness of that night in the Methodist Church, that as Mr. Bliss with his face radiant with unearthly joy was singing his own verse, spontaneously all those who had before asked prayer, rose to express their hope,—

> There's a part in that chorus for you and for me,
> And the theme of our praises for ever will be—
> Hallelujah, 'tis done ! I believe on the Son !
> I am saved by the blood of the Crucified One !

---

* The Hymn and Tune form No. 106 of " SACRED SONGS AND SOLOS."

Such scenes must be felt and witnessed in their reality to be understood. They are unhappily imitated by those who would see the effect without having inspired it by their own communion with the Holy Ghost. It is then that the thing looks mechanical, and scoffers are hardened. Oh, how holy and jealous of ourselves should we be, who do the Lord's work. Our desire to witness the success of our message, to prove our own power, leaves a loop-hole for Satan to neutralize our work, and hinders the power of the Spirit. We must not, however, shrink from Mr. Bliss's pronounced and outspoken enthusiasm in our Lord's work. Men of the world who rejoice to see men spring to their feet at a political meeting in order to express their resolves, and who scorn the unhallowed excitement of pretence, are often very deeply moved when they witness the effects of genuine emotion under religious appeals. The secret of true power is having the right testimony, and then forgetting the messenger in mightly longings for the success of the message ! but this can only be learnt by being much alone with the Master.

The Meetings in Jackson closed November 21st, and Mr. Bliss came to Chicago to attend the Christian Convention called by Mr. Moody. During the session he gave an address upon the use of song in worship. At the prayer meeting of ministers in Farwell Hall, presided over by Mr. Moody, on the morning of November 24th, nearly a thousand ministers from all parts of the North-west were present. It was an unusually solemn and earnest gathering, and the intense spiritual feeling prevailing found fit expression through Mr. Bliss in song. That morning the representatives of more than four hundred churches formed an " Alliance for Prayer," and covenanted to unite in intercession for each other, until God poured out His Spirit among them. Mr. Bliss felt the scene very much, and his heart melted with praise as he witnessed hundreds of honoured pastors re-consecrating themselves humbly and tearfully to the work of "watching for souls." Seated at the organ, he sang, at Mr. Moody's request, his own hymn and music :—

> Do you see the Hebrew captive kneeling,
>   At morning, noon, and night, to pray?
> In his chamber he remembers Zion,
>   Though in exile far away.
>
> Are your windows open toward Jerusalem,
>   Though as captives here a " little while " we stay?
> For the coming of the King in His glory,
>   Are you watching day by day? *

His face, it is recorded, fairly shone as he sang, and tears fell from hundreds of eyes. One devoted minister exclaimed, "God bless Mr. Bliss for that song;" and "Amen" came from all parts of the building. Never were the words sung with such a prophet-like grandeur of tone—

> " For the coming of the King in His glory,
>   Are you watching day by day ?"

Mr. Moody leaned forward in his chair, overcome by the emotion of the hour, and the realization of the Lord's coming and "the gathering together unto Him." It was the last time Mr. Moody was to hear Mr. Bliss on this side the river. He will hear his splendid voice again amid the radiance of the heavenly choir. Farwell Hall in Chicago had often witnessed the moving power of Mr. Bliss's words. That last appearance of his seemed to not a few a sort of transfiguration scene, and formed a very impressive close of his public work in that place hallowed by rich blessings and memories.

---

* "LATER SONGS AND SOLOS," No. 167.

Chapter VIII.

N November we again find Mr. Bliss in Peoria,
Illinois. Excellent brethren, such as Tyng,
McIlvaine, and Reynolds, were very cordial in
their welcome, and he and Mrs. Bliss were placed
under the hospitable care of Mr. and Mrs. R. Grier.
Rouse's Hall was kept full from night to night, and Christians were very active in their household visitations.

While the ministrations of Mr. Bliss and his colleague
were being successfully prosecuted, they were cheered by a
visit to that city of Mr. R. C. Morgan, of London. He
continued with them some days, and, anxious for the
furtherance of the work of God in England, laid before
them an invitation to visit the British Isles. Mr. Moody
had already urged the same call. The proposal was favourably looked upon by Mr. Bliss, and, with his wife and
helpers, guidance was sought in special prayer to the Father.
The intercourse then and on other occasions led Mr.
Morgan to say, " Mr. Bliss is my ideal of a Christian gentleman ; the most perfect specimen I ever met." At this time
the united pastors of Chicago were meeting to join in an
invitation to Mr. Bliss and Major Whittle to come there,
and follow up the wonderful results of Mr. Moody's services.

Mr. Bliss had his doubts as to the wisdom of this. Invitations from other places were also coming in, but his thoughts ran in the direction of the proposed visit to England. Mrs. Bliss was disposed to leave her children in the States. She said, " They are under as good care with our sister as they could possibly be. They love her now as much as they do me, and I believe it would be better for them and better for us in the work, if they are left in Rome." In commenting upon this, the remark was made that if accident should occur and we were drowned, the children would be safe. Her reply was, "Well, I should not think of that. If we ask the Lord to guide us, and it seems best for all to go, and we are all drowned, it is all right. It is the Lord's will, and it will be best. We should all go together." There were many who afterwards recalled those words.

In Peoria Mr. Bliss held his children's meetings each afternoon in the Methodist Church, and became more interested than ever in the work for the young, earnestly expressing his determination to labour more and more in that direction. He wrote a short time before this : " I would rather have a little girl or boy smile in my face and say, ' I think you are real good,' which means, ' I think you are something like Jesus,' than have a column of high-sounding praise in every newspaper in Chicago." A number of very interesting conversions among the young at this period gave him much pleasure. One dear little German boy, a manly little fellow of eight years old, interested Mr. and Mrs. Bliss very much. He was an intelligent child, and had a business-like way of speaking of his having accepted Christ, that commended him specially to Mrs. Bliss, who was always repelled by affectation in young or old. Since their death the following letter was received from their little Peoria friend. It is given verbatim :—

" Peoria, Ill., *January* 27, 1877.

"Dear Brother Whittle,—I saw a piece in the *Standard* about you and Mr. Bliss. I saw that you and Mr. Morgan, of London, were getting up a book of the Life of Mr. and Mrs. Bliss, and wanted to have letters from those who have been blessed or converted by his songs. I can say that I was converted when they was singing the second hymn, ' Hallelujah, 'tis Done.' In singing the chorus of it, I thought, ' Do I believe on the Son?' and so, as you gave the first invitation for all who were not Christians and wanted to be prayed for to rise, and then asked how many wanted to settle it now to rise, I was among that lot that rose as there were forty or fifty, you said. I saw five or six that rose that were right behind me. I attended all of Mr. Bliss's Children's Meetings, as also I attended all of yours. It was Thanksgiving Night, at the Centennial Hall, in which I was converted. I expect you know me. I am eight years old.—I remain, as ever, your friend,

" William B. H."

Mr. Reynolds writes from Peoria, in connection with Mr. Bliss's labours, that over fifty scholars in his Sunday School testified that they attributed the influence leading to their decision for Christ to his influence. In the evening meetings for adults, God gave him also many souls in Peoria. One night he was the last one home, and as he hung up his coat in the hall he remarked, in his happy way, " My last inquiry meeting was at the gate. Three dear young men, all hungry for the Gospel, and two of them have taken Christ."

His last visit in Peoria was made to the afflicted. To a weary one under heavy bereavement he sang his " I am tired;" and to a feeble and suffering girl in another home, " Crossing the tide."

About this time he received an account of a missionary's wife in Japan. She had gone out with her husband, Mr. True, and had felt the desolation of widowhood in that far-off heathen land, but had nobly resolved to continue at the post with her one little girl, to carry forward as she could the plans of her late husband and herself for the salvation of the people. With tears in his eyes, Mr. Bliss read the letter, and added, "We should be ashamed of ourselves if we ever spoke again of 'sacrifice' after this." The same day he ordered his publishers to forward a hundred books to the missionary's widow, for the school where she was teaching English. There came a letter from the grateful one; but he had heard, even before it was written, the great On-looker's words, "Inasmuch as ye have done it unto one of the least of these My brethren, ye have done it unto Me." The letter has a tender interest, and is here given :—

"No. 12, GINZA SANCHOME, TOKIO, *Jan.* 1, 1877.

"PROF. P. P. BLISS :

"DEAR BROTHER,—Surely it is a pleasant thing to be able to begin this new year by writing a letter of thanks.

"We had our Christmas festivities on the 26th, as we could not prepare in one day, and our school-rooms are also our church ; so we did not wish to decorate on Saturday. There were more than three hundred persons present, and nearly all were Japanese. For this I was very thankful, as it furnished the opportunity to tell many for the first time of our Saviour's wondrous love.

"I retired exceedingly weary, but glad in heart, because I believed the Master was pleased with our efforts to spread the news of His love. Before I arose next morning, a servant announced at my door, "Americano yubin" (American mail) ! He knew full well that, notwithstanding my fatigue, I would wish to know at once the glad tidings. I hastened to see what was in store for me, and to my *surprise* and *joy*, there were the 'Hymn Books.' I cannot tell you how glad I was, but I told our Father, and I am sure He will return a hundred-fold. At morning worship we had a thanksgiving service, and afterward the girls and I had a 'sing.' I wish you could have seen their happy faces, as they saw the nice new books, and turned at once to find 'Whosoever will.' They had learned that from my one copy, and sang it the evening before. But there were *so many!* What was intended? There was no letter to explain, and I could not wait a whole month to know, and so I just said we will share our joy with the other three schools in our mission. I gave a part to Miss Youngman, who has a girls' school, and some to Mr. Ballagh, who has a boys' school in Yokohama, and sent some to Miss Marsh for her school, also in Yokohama. That leaves a nice supply for us, and we sing and sing until we are hoarse. I hope I have not done wrong with them. The others were delighted, and you may be sure that your name and songs will be well known in our mission in Japan at least.   "MARIA T. TRUE."

Some of the facts respecting the generosity and disinterestedness of Mr. Bliss are very significant, as showing how completely the Lord had breathed His own Spirit into him. Says Dr. Goodwin :—

"He had what I fear comparatively few Christians have, a CHARITY FUND, to which he sacredly devoted a given part of his income. I do not know what that proportion was, but it has come to my knowledge that on occasion it yielded a thousand dollars in six months. No matter what needs pressed, that fund was never invaded. And the significant thing about it was that it never seemed to run dry. He has put repeatedly into my hands sums ranging from ten to twenty-five dollars to be used among the poor. And when

I expressed surprise at his being able to spare it, his reply was that God was very good to him and he never lacked. I have known him to hand his pocket-book to our church visitor after some recital of suffering or destitution, and tell her to help herself in behalf of those in need. I suspect that when the 'charity fund' failed through the demands upon it, there was a fresh assignment of income. Would that more of the Lord's people would follow this practice!"

The end was drawing nigh. The Lord was about to remove him from that earthly sphere in which he had been conformed to Himself. His noble unselfishness fitted him for the higher community of the perfected ones. A foreshadowing of the end seemed now to be upon him.

One day, while taking a walk that was almost a daily one with Mr. Bliss and Major Whittle, they spoke of the time when one of them would be walking alone, and thinking of the departed one in places where they had been together. He always was thinking of "the glorious appearing," and said, "Just as probable that Christ may come, and we all go together. What a beautiful day this would be for Him to come!" Then they talked of the sudden death of Mr. Moody's brother, and he spoke in tones that were almost premonitory of what was to come.

On December 14, Mr. Bliss and Major Whittle held their last Meeting together. From 8.30 a.m. to 5 p.m., with intermission at noon, they held a Christian Convention. Mr. Bliss sang through the day, and spoke with his usual earnestness and power.

In the evening, accompanied by Mr. R. C. Morgan, of London, who had spent the day with them, they went to Rouse's Hall. On the way Mr. Bliss remarked, "Major, if you want to sing 'Waiting and Watching' to-night, you must not say anything before asking me to sing. It is all that I can do to control my feelings, and if you introduce it by remarks, I shall break down." Mr. and Mrs. Bliss sang this piece, and " I Know not the Hour when my Lord will Come," that evening, the last hymn they were heard to sing together. Mr. Bliss sang alone, "Oh, the clanging Bells of Time ! " *

That evening they left for Chicago. They breakfasted and dined with Mr. Moody at the Brevoort House, and made preparations to journey to Rome, Penn., and then return to the West. Mr. Bliss, however, from the first had an almost unaccountable aversion to the plan proposed of his returning, from his Christmas visit to his children, to work in Chicago. He desired to remain in the East, evangelizing in New England, while Mr. Moody and Mr. Sankey were doing the same in Boston. Though unconvinced, he yielded, and it was arranged that he should go to Pennsylvania, and return to Chicago for the last day of the year.

Before leaving the hotel for this journey, the two faithful friends and evangelists knelt together before the Lord and committed their way to Him. Alas ! they were not to meet again till they clasped "inseparable hands" among the immortals. He passed the following Sunday in Towanda, Penn., with his mother, and his sister Mrs. Wilson. Thence he wrote to his coadjutor, who had returned to Peoria :—

" TOWANDA, *December* 17, 1876.

" DEAR WHITTLE,—We are within ten miles of the boys ; arrived here at two o'clock this morning, four hours late ; so are spending this Lord's-day with my sister, where my dear old mother is ' waiting.' I am glad for a day with her who gave me my first music lesson. And she is enjoying our visit so much. We remember you in our morning

* " LATER SONGS AND SOLOS," No. 184.

prayers.   Suppose Chicago is all settled.   Nevertheless my feeling is the same ; though my faith, I hope, is stronger. If He says 'Go!' I am ready.

"N.B.—The Lord is your Shepherd.   He will carry you through.   Hope your wife is better.   Dear child! may the Lord bless her to-day!   We hope to go to Rome to-morrow. Shall look for a letter from you soon.   I hope the Lord will lead the meeting at Peoria.   Give our regards to the 'singers, as well as the players upon instruments' who are there.   Also to the Grier House, Tyngs, Reynolds, and others.

> "'In peace I go,
> No fear I know.'

Wish you the same.

"P. P."

He wrote two other letters, which told of the joy he had felt on seeing his mother again, of the unbroken peace that filled her soul, and of the blessing her faith and prayers were to him.

Monday, December 18th, he rode by stage to Rome, Penn., and the parents were with their dear little boys again. For both of them all of the associations of home clustered around Father Young's house, their frequent happy resting-place on life's journey ; they came with joy to it now, both almost as merry as their little boys.   They had been purchasing and making articles for Christmas presents for weeks, and came with a trunk full of "surprises" for the approaching holiday.   When Christmas came, Ma Bliss * was sent for, and all the family circle within reach were gathered at the old home.   Mr. Bliss was the "Santa Claus." On Saturday he went out to the hillside and cut the Christ-

---

* Then Grandma Bliss.

mas tree, and with his own hands arranged it in the parlour
and hung his "surprises." On Monday morning the presents
were distributed, and " the happiest Christmas he had ever
known," as he said, was quickly passed. He had "surprises"
for everybody, and spent the day in making everybody
happy. From Grandma Allen,* down to little George, everybody in the entire circle was remembered, and " portions
were sent" outside the circle to all of whom he could learn
in the village as being in want.† He himself was not without his " surprises." Gifts from the wife and other loved ones,
and a magnificent music box from his loved friend and pub-
lisher, Mr. Church, added to his happiness.

This Christmas was to him the crowning joy and mercy
of a year of mercies. His affectionate heart overflowed
with thankfulness to God and with earnest desire to do more
in the service of the Saviour. He visited nearly every day
among the neighbours, and urged the claims of Christ upon
the personal attention of those unsaved. He attended
nearly every meeting, and sang and gave Bible readings,
and made personal appeals to his friends to decide at once
for Christ. All testify that they never knew him more loving
and earnest. Grandma Allen says : " He would come in
and say, ' Grandma, I wish I could see every person in this
valley a Christian.' " The account " Grandma " gave of a
home meeting on one of the last days, when they gathered
for a Bible talk, will illustrate the enjoyment her originality
gave him. She said : " He had been asking them all
around where they would have chosen to have seen Jesus,
when He was on the earth, if they had to select one place.
They fixed on different places, and he said he would rather
have seen Him as He went up into heaven from the Mount
of Olives ; and then asked me where I should like to have

---

* Then Great-Grandma. † Practically carrying out Neh. viii. 10.

seen Him, and I told him that I had rather have seen Him when He was a little helpless baby, there in the manger, among the oxen, and helped to take care of Him; and he just cried about it."

God blessed Mr. Bliss's testimony and labour during this last week to the conversion of many old friends and neighbours, and others now acknowledge that they owe their decision to his influence, and that the light they received from the Son of God came through him.

Mr. Bliss's last Meeting was held Wednesday evening, December 27th. He was full of the Holy Spirit, and sang with more than usual power. Among the pieces that friends remember as sung that night are—"Alas! and did my Saviour Bleed?" to the tune of Dundee; "Happy Day!" and "In the Christian's Home in Glory." He sang as solos "Eternity," "Father, I'm Tired," and as a closing song, "Hold Fast till I Come." In singing "Father, I'm Tired," he took occasion to speak of Major Whittle, his companion in the work, and of his affection for him, and that he would sing the piece because it was one of his favourites. The last song, probably, that he sang on earth was "Hold Fast till I Come." He prefaced his singing it by saying that it was one of the first occasions of its being sung, and that it might be the last hymn he should ever sing to them.

The *last* music from the pen of Mr. Bliss was written for the following hymn, to which he added the chorus. Surely in the light of what has since transpired, we may say there was a teaching of the Divine Spirit of the change that was at hand as he lingered over the words:—

> " I know not what awaits me,
>   God kindly veils mine eyes,
> And o'er each step of my onward way
>   He makes new scenes to rise;
> And every joy He sends me comes
>   A sweet and glad surprise.

Where He may lead I'll follow,
  My trust in Him repose ;
And ev'ry hour in perfect peace
  I'll sing—" He knows, He knows."

One step I see before me,
  'Tis all I need to see ;
The light of heaven more brightly shines,
  When earth's illusions flee ;
And sweetly through the silence comes
  His loving " Follow Me ! "

O blissful lack of wisdom !
  'Tis blessed not to know :
He holds me with His own right hand,
  And will not let me go ;
And lulls my troubled soul to rest
  In Him who loves me so.

So on I go, not knowing,
  I would not if I might ;
I'd rather walk in the dark with God
  Than go alone in the light ;
I'd rather walk by faith with Him
  Than go alone by sight." *

Major Whittle writes, and his words are the best in which to record the end :—

"On Wednesday, a letter came to me from Mr. Bliss, in which he said :—' I hear nothing from you definite as to my being wanted in Chicago next Sunday. Unless I hear from you, I shall not leave this week.' This letter came in the morning. We had been advertised to sing in Mr. Moody's Tabernacle the following Sunday afternoon. It was necessary to telegraph him to come. But evening came and found me at my home, and the telegram was not sent. I had not forgotten it, but did not want to send it. I did

---

* This hymn, written by Miss M. G. Brainerd, has been erroneously attributed to Mr. Bliss.

not know then, I do not know now, why. All day long it was upon my mind, and was spoken of to friends, that Bliss must be telegraphed for, and that I did not like to take the responsibility of doing it. Late in the evening, the despatch was forwarded.

"Thursday morning, he took his little boys into a room by themselves and prayed with them, bade "Good-bye" to all, and, standing upon the threshold for a moment, said, 'I should love to stay. I would far rather stay than go, if it were God's will; but I must be about the Master's work.' He telegraphed back from Waverly, New York, a station on the Erie Railroad, the same afternoon, 'Tickets for Chicago, viâ Buffalo and Lake Shore Railroad. Baggage checked through. Shall be in Chicago Friday night. God bless you all for ever.'

"Taking the afternoon train at Waverly, he expected to be in Buffalo at twelve o'clock that night, and connect with a train that would arrive in Chicago Friday evening. Ten miles from Waverly (as I learned from the conductor, in tracing him up), the engine of the train broke, and they were detained three hours. Their connection with this train was thus lost; and upon arriving at Hornellsville late in the evening, they evidently decided to wait over, and have a night's rest, and arrive in Chicago Saturday morning at nine o'clock—for at Hornellsville they left the train, and are registered at the hotel, which they left Friday morning, taking the train which connected at Buffalo with the Chicago train, wrecked at Ashtabula, Ohio. The children were not with them, but had been left at Rome, Pennsylvania, in the care of grandparents and aunt."

The story of the disaster by which these two precious lives were lost will be found in another chapter. What experiences they passed through, in that night of fear and pain, we shall not know until we meet them on the other side.

MRS. P. P. BLISS.

From all the evidence that could be gathered from the testimony of survivors, it is believed that the Buffalo and Cleveland saloon car, in which they were seen by Mr. Burchell, also by a lady passenger, and by the newsboy of the train, struck first upon the ice after the fall of the bridge, and that another car fell upon it, crushing and probably instantly killing the passengers within. The floor of this car was identified in removing the wreck, and lay flat upon the ice, with the water that had come from the melted snow and ice, mingled with ashes and cinders, frozen over it, thus confirming the above theory.

Major Whittle continues :—

"Saturday morning, December 30, when I read the report of the disaster, my heart sank within me, and I feared the worst. I immediately telegraphed to Rome to know if Mr. Bliss had left. But about three o'clock in the afternoon, before any reply from Rome, Mr. Burchell's telegram came, and we were face to face with the awful fact of their death. The next morning we were at Ashtabula, and remained for three days, until all the wreck had been removed, searching first for their bodies, then for anything that could be identified as having been connected with them. We found nothing ; and up to this time nothing has been found. Their watches, sleeve-buttons, chains, keys, rings, not one thing connected with them has come to light. Scores of such articles have been raked up from the bottom of the river, but none of them are theirs. They have gone, as absolutely and completely gone, as if translated like Enoch.

"Of the meeting with the stricken households, and the dear orphan boys, and the days of mourning passed with them, I cannot speak. God graciously manifested Himself in the comfort vouchsafed to the aged parents, and to brothers and sisters who shared their grief, and it was better indeed to be 'in the house of mourning than the house of feasting.' Some of the number there gathered were led to consecrate themselves to the work of Christ, and are now engaged in prosecuting the work of the dear departed brother in singing the gospel. Many at the service for the dead held in Rome were led to accept of Christ, and from all over the land has come testimony that Christ has been magnified in the death of His child as in his life. Very many by the very fact of his death, have been impressed and turned to God. Hundreds will receive the truth through the pathos of memory of his death, giving new meaning to the truth of his songs—'God's ways are always right.' No mistake has been made. We bow in submission to His will, and pray that this afflictive providence may be sanctified to us by the Spirit of God, and that, with 'windows open toward Jerusalem,' we may live day by day, ready for 'the coming of the King in His beauty,' or for our departure to be with Him. 'Amen, even so, come quickly, Lord Jesus.'

"Farewell, dear friend and brother, true yoke-fellow in the service of Jesus Christ! The path of life is often lonely without you, and as others sing the songs you used to sing, and we listen in vain for the voice so wedded to the music, and music so wedded to the words, our hearts ache as the echoes die away, and a strange silence is on the air, as if the song itself mourned for the singer. No resting-place beneath the sod can receive the tears we would shed, or the flowers we would bring to tell how we loved thee. We turn from the earthly memories to the heavenly realities. The days are fast passing by; soon upon the other shore we shall greet you; and you shall lead our praises to Him who hath redeemed us from our sins by His shed blood, and in His risen life hath given us resurrection hope, and to whom, even to Jesus our Lord, we now give all the praise for every sweet memory and for every precious anticipation of future meeting with you, and every joy associated with your name!"

Chapter IX.

THE DISASTER AT ASHTABULA.

BEFORE proceeding to notice the memorial services and the testimonies to Mr. Bliss's character, the circumstances of the railway accident by which Mr. and Mrs. Bliss were killed are here interposed, for the information of English readers who may not know the terrible details.

The scene of the accident was the valley of the creek which, flowing past the village of Ashtabula, Ohio, goes under the railway three or four hundred yards east of the station. Over this there was an iron structure, with a single span of 159 feet, crossed by a double track seventy feet above the water, which at that time was covered with ice. The train in which Mr. and Mrs. Bliss travelled left Buffalo, New York, on Friday afternoon, Dec. 29, 1876; and a despatch to Chicago relates :—

" The disaster occurred shortly before eight o'clock. It was the wildest winter night of the year. Three hours behind its time, the Pacific express, which had left New York the night before, struggled along through the drifts and the blinding storm. The eleven cars were a heavy burden to the two engines ; and when the leading locomotive broke through the drifts beyond the ravine, and rolled on across the bridge, the train was moving at less than ten miles an

hour.   The head-lamp threw but a short and dim flash of
light in the front, so thick was the air with the driving snow.
The train crept across the bridge, the leading engine had
reached solid ground beyond, and its driver had just given
it steam, when something in the undergearing of the bridge
snapped.   For an instant there was a confused crackling of
beams and girders, ending with a tremendous crash, as the
whole train, except the leading engine, broke through the
framework, and fell in a heap of crushed and splintered
ruins at the bottom.   Notwithstanding the wind and storm,
the crash was heard by people within doors half a mile away.
For a moment there was silence, a stunned sensation among
the survivors, who, in all stages of mutilation, lay piled
among the dying and dead.   Then arose the cries of the
maimed and suffering ; the few who remained unhurt hastening to escape from the shattered cars.

   " Five minutes after the train fell, the fire broke out in
the cars piled against the abutments at either end.   A moment later flames arose from the smoking-car and the first
carriage, piled across each other near the middle of the
stream.   In less than ten minutes after the catastrophe
every car in the wreck was on fire ; and the flames, fed by
the dry varnished work, and fanned by the icy gale, licked
up the ruins as though they had been tinder.   Destruction
was so swift, that mercy was baffled.   Men who, in the
bewilderment of the shock, sprang out and reached the
solid ice, went back after wives and children, and found
them suffocating in the flames.   The neighbouring residents,
startled by the crash, were lighted to the scene by the con-
flagration, which made even their prompt assistance too
late.   By midnight the destruction was complete.   The
storm had subsided, but the wind still blew fiercely, and the
cold was more intense.   When morning came, all that remained of the Pacific express was a chaos of car-wheels,

axles, brake-irons, truck-frames, and twisted rails, lying in a black pool at the bottom of the gorge. The wood had burned completely away, and the ruins were covered with white ashes."

Of the hundred and sixty passengers, only fifty-nine could be found or accounted for.

Mr. J. E. Burchell, of Chicago, was one of the survivors, and gives the following account :—

"We neared the bridge at about 7.25, though due at Ashtabula at 5.15. We ran on to the structure at a rate of about ten miles an hour, and the whole train was on the bridge when it gave way. The bridge was about two hundred feet long, and only the first engine had passed over when the crash came, the weight of the falling cars nearly pulling back the locomotive that had passed over.

"The first thing I heard was a cracking in the front part of the car, and the same cracking in the rear. Then came another cracking in the front louder than the first, and then came a sickening oscillation and a sudden sinking, and I was thrown stunned from my seat. The iron work bent and twisted like snakes, and everything took horrid shapes.

"The train lay in the valley in the water, our car a little on its side, both ends broken in. The rest of the train lay in every direction, some on end, some on the side, crushed and broken, a terrible sight. Below were the water and broken ice ; and seventy feet above was the broken bridge.

"The snow in the valley was nearly to my waist, and I could only move with difficulty. The wreck was then on fire. The wind was blowing from the east and whirling blinding masses of snow over the terrible ruin.

"I did not then know that any lives had been lost. The fire stole swiftly along the wreck, and in a few moments the cars were all in flames. The ruins covered the whole space between the two piers, the cars jammed in or locked together. One engine lay in the creek, smashed to pieces, the ruins breathing steam and fire.

"I carried a lady to the only house near by, and which appeared to be an engine-house. I was completely exhausted, and did not go back to the wreck, but from the engine-house door I could see into the ravine, and the fearful scene it presented. The whole wreck was then on fire, and from out the frozen valley came great bursts of flame. The spectacle was frightful, but those who had gone to assist worked steadily in spite of the intense heat. Physicians and surgeons were early at hand, and every effort was made to relieve the sufferers. I did not know the name of one of the killed except Mr. and Mrs. Bliss.

"When the train fell, Mr. Bliss succeeded in crawling through a window, supposing he could pull his wife after him. But she was jammed fast, and every effort of his was unavailing. The car was all jammed up, and the lady was caught in the ironwork of the seats. Finding that he could not save her, he stayed there with her and died."

This concluding statement of Mr. Burchell may be literally true—it would have been like Mr. Bliss's generous nature ; but it is possible that the actual circumstances of the death were somewhat different. Such a scene of awful excitement is not favourable to exactitude, and the final end must be left under the painful mystery which shrouds it.

Chapter X.

"BE STILL, AND KNOW THAT I AM GOD."—*Psalm* xlvi. 10.

ITH the word "mystery" the last chapter closed. By this is meant no more than that "Now we see through a glass darkly." "Now we know in part." The profound must have in it an aspect of mystery. The attempt to

> "Assert eternal Providence,
> And justify the ways of God to men,"

is not for mortals. "The goal of this great world lies beyond sight." The human race by whom Incarnate love in the Person of the Son of God was crucified, and to whom the cross of His suffering becomes the Fount of salvation, must accept the inexplicable till we see "face to face, and know even as we are known." Meanwhile we know this: the lesson of patient trust is the supreme lesson of life. "It is not fitting that servants," to quote a weighty thought of a heathen in a letter of Xenophon to Æschines, "should know more respecting the plans of their lord than what the service of him requires." The proofs of Divine love, and that the Father of Jesus is "very pitiful and of tender mercy," are so overwhelming to an enlightened soul as to silence all doubt of the rectitude of His administration. It is not merely the Christian who is per-

plexed by the mystery of suffering; the sceptic is much
more so.   No utterances over the perplexities of life are so
terrible in their sadness as are those of modern doubters.
We Christians are prepared for insolvable difficulties.   We
take the place of children, whom the "Father of spirits" is
training by the trust, not of knowledge, but of faith.   The
long roll of the martyrs; the frustration of noble purposes;
the bitter anguish of the holiest of men and women; the
apparent triumph of evil workers,—are parts of a system
altogether beyond our understanding.   "The things revealed are for us;" the hidden things are with God, and
are parts of the method whereby our Almighty Father is
educating us in the loyalty of an implicit and unfaltering
confidence in Himself.   We become better, holier, and
stronger, when in our heart of hearts we hear the word,
—"Be still, and know that I am God."   "Here is the
patience of the saints."

As to those two prepared ones, may not the angel of
Providence have allowed the human catastrophe to work its
consequences on them because "heaven is attracting to
itself whatever is congenial to its nature"?   Dr. J. H. Vincent, of Plainfield, New York, has admirably written :—

"That tempest was to our dear Bliss and his wife the
'whirlwind' in which they were caught up, as by a 'chariot
of fire,' into the kingdom of the Eternal.   Whether killed
by the fall, or the waters, or the fire, it mattered little to
them.   Whether the struggle was for but a moment, or
protracted for many minutes, it was for them to look
the dear Lord in the face—the Lord whom they had
trusted and loved so long—and all was well !   And all now
is well !

"How can we account for such a wonderful visitation?
Are good men so plentiful that the Lord can remove one so

useful just at the time of his largest promise? What *does* it all mean?

"Well, we are not called upon to explain it. But we do see a few things in the visitation which give us some light and consolation.

"1. The departed brother and his wife were ready. They were ripe for heaven. Why should we mourn or wonder when the chorus of the skies is made stronger and sweeter?

"2. The songs our dear brother wrote are still with us. And they have received a new sweetness and significance and power by the tragic end of the singer of them.

"3. This death has startled into new activity and con-secration the workers in all the churches. Who can esti-mate the intensified convictions, the strengthened purposes, the redoubled diligence, among that blessed brotherhood who are at work in Christendom?—and all this, under God, caused by this solemn call.

"4. By the peculiar method of the Divine Providence in the present case, a holy Christian life is brought before the public. Brother Bliss now preaches with a tongue of fire to the millions. Tens of thousands who had never seen nor even heard of the departed are now brought face to face with his lovely character, and with the Christ he so faith-fully proclaimed.

"5. But is there no ministry in the sphere to which he has been removed for such a royal soul as his?

"Dear Bliss! The memories will come—his face, his noble form, his gentle manners, his fervent prayers and appeals, his deep absorption in the one beautiful work of his life! Farewell, dear friend! Our hearts bleed at the thought that we shall here see him no more! The world seems lonely without him! But we shall meet yonder."

Surely it is even as Dr. Vincent points out—a holy Christian life is brought before the public, and Mr. Bliss now preaches to tens of thousands who would not otherwise have heard of one in whom "joy in the Holy Ghost" was the atmosphere in which passion was subdued; in whose character such a sweetness, grace, and dignity of loveliness, grew up; and who rebuked vice, less by reproof, than by the contrast of his own beautiful life. And what is this blessing after death; but that which the Lord taught in His own suggestive figure?—" Except a corn of wheat fall into the ground and die, it remaineth alone; but if it die, it bringeth forth *much* fruit."

At no time since the great Evangelical revival of the last century has the Church so needed to be reminded of the spirit of the men and women who are in sympathy with the work of Mr. Bliss. Many have lost the impression of the rich and transcendent influence upon the daily walk of the realization of the Saviour's love. Doubters who have forgotten the lessons of the martyrdom of other days have come to think of Christianity as addressing itself to fear, and as finding its followers among the weak and timid. Even professors of religion have come to regard the sublime spirituality of the New Testament as depressing, and they turn to those doubtful pleasures which on all sides are multiplying their attractions and seductions.

At such a time, and to young men especially, who are the hope of society, the record of the noble manliness, and the fulness of joy of PHILIP BLISS, who, without a shade of cant or asceticism, threw himself heartily into his Christianity, will not be without its uses. Moreover, the history of one who rose from poverty to be a minister of praise; who sought to lead the human heart out of itself to a boundless trust in the mercy and grace of man's Divine Friend and Redeemer, will indicate, in the days of trial that are at hand, where are those places of communion and of triumph of which we have to say,—" It is good to be here."

Deeply conscious is the writer of this English Edition how inadequately he has conveyed the impression which the records of the brief career of Mr. Bliss have left upon his own mind; and how God "anointed him with the oil of gladness"; but enough may have been done to show what blessed results will come to the Church in these last days, when the spirit of praise for all the wonders of redeeming love fills its borders. "Let the people praise Thee, O God; let all the people praise Thee. Then shall the earth yield her increase; and God, even our own God, shall bless us." (Ps. lxvii. 5, 6.)

With the sweet verses of Mr. Bliss we may appropriately close this chapter. In "LATER SONGS AND SOLOS" are the lines, with Mr. Bliss's music :—

TO DIE IS GAIN.

"To die is gain :"
All earthly cares forsaking,
From toil and pain,
To endless joy awaking :
To die is gain.

"To die is gain :"
My weary soul home bringing;

O'er heavenly plain,
Sweet angel voices singing :
To die is gain.

"To die is gain :"
From strife and sin to sever,
With Christ to reign,
For ever, oh, for ever :
To die is gain.

In another of his books of Sunday-school music are words which come from him to us who remain :—

Only a few more years,
Only a few more cares ;
Only a few more smiles and tears,
Only a few more prayers :

Only a few more wrongs,
Only a few more sighs ;

Only a few more earthly songs,
Only a few good-byes.

Then an eternal stay,
Then an eternal throng ;
Then an eternal glorious day,
Then an eternal song.

Chapter XXI.

HE following chapter consists of the Memorial Notice which appeared in *The Christian* of January 25, 1877. It is from the pen of its editor, Mr. R. C. Morgan, then in Chicago, and who had visited Mr. Bliss at Peoria only a few days before. The article was written in Chicago, to which city, as already stated, Mr. Bliss was on his way, after a few days' visit to his home in Pennsylvania, with the intention of assisting in the great Meetings there, when the Ashtabula catastrophe took place.

"And devout men carried Stephen to his burial, and made great lamentation over him." Something of this kind has been repeated here. The lamentation is over two of the sweetest singers in Israel—Mr. and Mrs. P. P. Bliss—without even the mournful satisfaction of carrying them to their burial. I scarcely know how to write the sorrowful tidings which I have to send to-day. I had gone to Canada for Christmas week, and returned on Saturday night (December 30) to meet these friends in Jesus, and make some final arrangements as to their coming to England with Major Whittle in the spring. Though I had heard on the way of a frightful railway accident at Ashtabula, in Ohio, it did not occur to me that they would be travelling by that very train—the Pacific Express. But on arriving at Chicago I was appalled to hear that they had perished on the previous night.

At Peoria, in the State of Illinois, I spent a few days with them. Mr. Bliss was a saint indeed, and his wife a true helpmate to him. "A prince and a great man is fallen in Israel," and of him and his sweet wife it may well be added, "They were lovely and pleasant in their lives, and in their death they were not divided."

On Saturday night, Major Whittle, Mr. Farwell, Mr. Jacobs, and others, went to the scene of the accident, to endeavour to recover the remains, but a telegram to Mr. Moody says that most of the bodies recovered are quite unrecognizable; and there seems no likelihood of anything being found of this beloved brother and sister whom Chicago mourns, and whom thousands all over the land and through the world are mourning, and will mourn more deeply, as the hymns he wrote, and which they sang together, are more fully understood. Their bodies have probably been burned to ashes, but they are themselves transfigured, and to us the hymns are transfigured also. We have been saying one to another that, read in the light of this fiery translation, they seem all changed to prophecies. How differently shall we now sing—

> I know not the hour when my Lord shall come,
> To take me away to His own dear home,
> But I know that His presence will lighten the gloom,
>   And that will be glory for me.
>
> I know not the form of my mansion fair,
> I know not the name that I then shall bear;
> But I know that my Saviour will welcome me there,
>   And that will be heaven for me.

After the Chicago fire he wrote and dedicated to Mr. Moody the words and music, "Roll on, O billow of fire!" the chorus of which must have come back with even more vividness in the fire in which he perished than when written in recollection of the fire from which he had escaped.

How much more tenderly shall we now sing that child-like carol which was the one that took the earliest hold of us at home—

> I am so glad that our Father in heaven
> Tells of His love in the Book He has given.
> Wonderful things in the Bible I see ; ·
> This is the dearest—that Jesus loves me.

It melts one's heart to think how, in the agony of that last hour, the husband and wife needed to cling, as to an anchor within the vail, to the assurance that, even in this terrible ordeal, " Jesus loves me."

After a visit to a beautiful cemetery in Peoria, and with his thoughts specially drawn toward the " blessed hope, and glorious appearing of the great God and our Saviour Jesus Christ," Mr. Bliss wrote—

> Down life's dark vale we wander,
>   Till Jesus comes ;

and although the death of the individual is not the coming of the Lord to receive His bride to Himself, yet what a sublime fulfilment did those simple lines receive on that dreadful night !

> He'll know what griefs oppressed me,
>   When Jesus comes.
> Oh, how His arms will rest me,
>   When Jesus comes.

And now that he is gone, how inspiriting will be the war-song, as we think how, trusting in the living God, he held the fort in death !—

> Ho, my comrades, see the signal
>   Waving in the sky !
> Reinforcements now appearing,
>   Victory is nigh.

" Hold the fort, for I am coming ! "
　　Jesus signals still,
　Wave the answer back to heaven—
　　" By thy grace we will."

A story was recently told of a missionary in South Africa
going into a kraal to rest, and the first sounds he heard were
from a Zulu singing this tune.　So these stirring strains go
round the world.

As we remember how our noble brother stood, and how
he fell, shall we not mean something more than ever before
in singing?—

　　Dare to be a Daniel !
　　　Dare to stand alone !
　　Dare to have a purpose firm !
　　　Dare to make it known !

To us here,* it seems as if his patient and truthful voice
were singing out of the darkness and terror of that wintry
storm—

　　Brightly beams our Father's mercy,
　　　From His lighthouse evermore ;
　　But to us He gives the keeping
　　　Of the lights along the shore ;

and that he appeals, with outstretched hands, on behalf of
others—

　　Let the lower lights be burning,
　　　Send the gleam across the wave ;
　　Some poor fainting, struggling seaman
　　　You may rescue, you may save.

For he met his end not far from the very spot (Cleveland
harbour) where the catastrophe occurred, which, related by
Mr. Moody, was the occasion of his writing—

---

　* It will be remembered that this was written at Chicago.

> Trim your feeble lamp, my brother,
>   Some poor seaman, tempest-tost,
> Trying now to make the harbour,
>   In the darkness may be lost.

We might almost trace the growth of his inner life in his experimental hymns. We note the steps of his conversion in the life-story so briefly yet so fully told in the one beginning :

> A long time I wandered in darkness and sin ;

and which is summed up in the lines :

> I *wished* He were mine ; yes, I *wished* He were mine,
> And then began *hoping* that Jesus was mine,
> I'm hoping no longer, I *know* He is mine.

In the same vein of advancing experience, we have the grand utterance, yet simple as a nursery rhyme :

> Free from the law, oh, happy condition !
> Jesus hath bled, and *there* is remission !
> Cursed by the law, and bruised by the fall,
> Grace hath redeemed us once for all.

At the Industrial Exposition at Chicago it was an every-day appointment, " Meet me at the Fountain." Our sweet singer, his mind always set on the things above, caught up the words and wrote—

> Will you meet me at the fountain,
>   When I reach the glory-land ?
> Will you meet me at the fountain,
>   Shall I clasp your friendly hand ?
> Other friends will give me welcome,
>   Other loving voices cheer ;
> There'll be music at the fountain,
>   Will you, will you meet me there ?

I spent but a few days in his society, but the impression

he has left upon my heart is well expressed in the question
and the assurance—

> Will you meet me at the fountain ?
> I shall long to have you near,
> When I meet my loving Saviour,
> When His welcome words I hear.

And so I might go on, for "Still there's more to
follow."

> Oh, the grace the Father shows ;
> Oh, the love that Jesus shows ;
> Oh, the power the Spirit shows !

This was his experience, and although the flow of his
sweet melodies is stayed on earth, before the throne—drinking of the water of life which proceeds from the throne of
God and the Lamb—he will praise on through the long day
of his eternal life ; and the refrain of the unfinished song
through the ages to come will be—

> Still there's more to follow.

Perhaps it is well that the stream of song has been
diverted to the heavenly land. We might have gone on
asking for some new thing, thinking more of the songs than
of the salvation of which they speak, and forgetting the
Giver in the gift. Therefore the only wise God our Saviour
has transfigured those we have, and shown us depths of
sacred tenderness, and love, and courage, that we had only
dimly seen before ; and, thus enriching the songs we possess, He has caught up the singer to His throne and heart,
while we are left to urge them that are

> Almost persuaded now to believe,
> Almost persuaded Christ to receive,

to yield, and say—

> Fully persuaded, Jesus is mine :
> Fully persuaded, Lord, I am thine.

And as one by one saved souls confess the Saviour's name, our departed friend will remember that he said, and by the grace of God fulfilled his pledge—

> Surely my Captain may depend on me,
> Though but an armour-bearer I may be.

Now he is gone, and his memory is very fragrant. We may write his epitaph in the words of Dr. Bonar's hymn, which Mr. Bliss had set to music, and the second verse of which is peculiarly suitable, and true of his most unselfish life—

> So, in the harvest, if others may gather
> Sheaves from the fields that in spring I have sown ;
> Who ploughed or sowed matters not to the reaper :
> I'm only remembered by what I have done.

And no doubt can remain on any heart that there has been a full and blessed answer to the aspiration, which he had set to sweetest strains—

> And when, with my glorified vision, at last
> The walls of "that city" I see,
> Will any one then at the Beautiful Gate
> Be waiting and watching for me?

"I heard a voice from heaven saying unto me, Write, Blessed are the dead which die in the Lord from henceforth : Yea, saith the Spirit, that they may rest from their labours ; and their works do follow them." (Rev. xiv. 13.)

Chapter XII.

Memorial Services at Rome and Chicago—Addresses by Dr. Goodwin—
Mr. Moody—Services in the Tabernacle.

N Sunday, January 7, 1877, Memorial Services were held in Rome, Pennsylvania. Sleighs from all directions were seen at break of that wintry day coming down the slopes of the hills, and bearing on them the sorrowful countenances of relatives and friends. It was a mournful day in that village, where the two were known so well. Among the mourners was the venerable mother of the poet-musician, with his sisters, and their husbands; "Grandma Allen," whose treasured dollars had made it possible for the "country boy" to pursue his taste for music; the stricken father and mother of Mrs. Bliss, with brothers and their wives, sisters and their husbands. The circle of relatives was large; and, pleasant to record, there was not one of them who was not a professed believer in the Lord. By eleven o'clock the Presbyterian Church was crowded in every part. A thick shade of deep and tearful sadness rested on the assembly. The pastor of a neighbouring Methodist church announced the hymn of Dr. Watts—"God is the Refuge of His Saints." Mr. McGranahan, well known in musical circles, led the singing. After prayer by another neighbouring pastor, Toplady's "Rock of Ages" was sung to the music composed by Mrs. Bliss. Their devoted and tried friend, Major Whittle, then gave a history of his visit to the scene of the accident, adding the words, " And we are left here to-day with nothing of these friends but the thought of them in glory."

Mr. Bliss's favourite hymn was then sung,—" I know not the hour when my Lord will come." The words, how- ever, so deeply taxed emotion, that the assembly was sub- dued; and Mr. McGranahan, the composer of the music, was so overcome, that sobs prevented the conclusion of the hymn.

Mr. and Mrs. Bliss were members, at the time of their death, of the first Congregational Church in Chicago, and their pastor, the Rev. Dr. E. P. Goodwin, gave the following appropriate and eloquent address : —

" My friends, I feel that I have come here as a kind of representative of that great family that to-day all through the land bows under the grief that has gathered us, and mingles its tears and prayers with those of this dear circle. Indeed, I seem almost to be a member of this household, so personal to me is this affliction. This dear brother had been for years one with whom I had wrought for the Master in most delightful accord. Our aims were one, our sympathies in unison, our friendship hearty ; and one of these precious children bears, as you may know, my name. Hence I come not to speak in any formal way, but out of the depths of my heart to utter a few words of loving tribute to one whose character and work I delight to honour.

" Let me connect what I have to say with two passages of Scripture, viz., Psalm cxvi. 15 : ' Precious in the sight of the Lord is the death of His saints.' Rev. xiv. 13 : ' And I heard a voice from heaven saying unto me, Write,

Blessed are the dead which die in the Lord from hence-forth ; yea, saith the Spirit, that they may rest from their labours ; and their works do follow them.'

" Dear friends, God makes no mistakes. The signi-ficance of God's providences does not lie in what we think of them, but in what God says about them. In His testi-mony we can alone find sure anchorage for faith, sure solace for bereavement. Our reasonings, apart from His Word, instead of scattering the darkness, often deepen it. We get rid of the gloom in a dark room when we open the shutters, and let the light shine in. And we get rid of the gloom that enwraps us in these trial-times of faith, when we stop arguing, and throw open the windows of our souls to the light of God's Word.

" The first thought, therefore, which I suggest in con-nection with this Providence is, that God's children are not to look upon death with dread, but to welcome it. If the death of God's saints is precious in His sight, and the day in which it comes better than the day of birth, surely His children need not be dismayed. Where God's face beams, our faces ought to brighten. Where God pronounces His benediction, and all the blessed of the Upper Presence join in special jubilee, we may at least dismiss our fears, and even though it be through tears, lift up our song.

" Even the Old Testament emphasizes this thought. There is something beautiful in the composure with which the old patriarchs laid aside their tent-life for the better country. How significant the record that they ' fell asleep,' ' were gathered to their fathers,' ' entered into rest.' What more touching and home-like, and free from everything like fear, than the picture of a father, conscious that his last hour is close at hand, calling his children about his bed-side, declaring the fact of his near departure, giving them his dying counsels and benediction, and then quietly wrapping his mantle about him, and lying down for the death-angel to close his eyes ! Take the death of Moses. First he was closeted with God. Then God rolled away the cloud from the mountain-top, touched his eyes, and gave him a vision of that fair land, in all its length and breadth, which he had so coveted to enter. When He took him, as it were, in His arms, as a mother would take a child,—and as the vision of the land of promise faded away,—there came instead the vision of that other country, even the heavenly, of which the earthly inheritance was but the feeble type ; and as its surpassing beauty burst upon his soul, he passed into the presence of the King, and was ' clothed upon ' with a transfiguring glory. Who of us would have drawn back dismayed from that dying hour, had it been permitted us to be there ?

"And this is the spirit of the Gospel. It knows nothing of depression or dismay as connected with the dying of God's people. On the contrary, every witness respecting it is of unqualified cheer. It is ' falling asleep,' ' entering into rest,' being ' present with the Lord.'

* * * * * *

"Our brother's anticipations of death were all of this unclouded, hopeful kind. You find no word of gloom in his Hymns, but when he touches the thought of death he almost invariably breaks out into a strain of peculiar exultation. Take that beautiful song, ' That will be Heaven for me,' sung in the opening service. It reads like a prophecy, and it exactly represents its author's feeling.

> "'I know not the hour when my Lord will come
> To take me away to His own dear home ;
> But I know that His presence will lighten the gloom,
> And that will be glory for me.'

"Or take that other still more prophetic song, ' There's a Light in the Valley ' :—

    "' I shall find down the valley no alarms,
      For my blessed Saviour's smile I can see ;
    He will bear me in His loving, mighty arms :
    There's a light in the valley for me.'

"Death, no matter what its form, had for Philip Bliss
no terrors. He believed with all his soul that Jesus Christ
came to 'abolish death,' to 'destroy him that had the power
of death—that is, the devil—and deliver them who through
fear of death were all their life-time subject to bondage.'
Hence, though living his life in the daily expectation that
the end might come, he was not only undismayed, but
overflowing with gladness.

"Turning now to some features of our brother's character which have impressed me, let me notice first, the
wonderful sunniness or hopefulness which marked his life.
I think I might safely call him the most joyous Christian I
have ever known. It was a rare thing to see a shadow even
transiently clouding his face. I remember when he came to
me with one of his Sunday School singing-books just ready
for the press, and desired help as to a fitting name. While
we were conversing, suddenly his countenance lighted up
with the words, 'I believe I have it : why not call it Sunshine ?' And some of you will recall how on the cover
there was emblazoned the full-orbed splendour of the sun.
So when the 'Gospel Songs' came out, the cover bore a
similar device, but with an open Bible in the heart of the
rays. No symbol could have been more apt. His life, if
not always lived under a clear sky, always had the sun
shining through the clouds.

"Not that he was exempt from trials. He had his
share of earthly disappointments, and the keen discipline they bring. He knew what it was to be misappre-
hended ; to have mean and selfish motives attributed to
him ; to be talked of as having a desire for self-glorification

in leading the praise-service of the sanctuary; to be accused
of singing for pay.   If any of you have known what it is
to have the conceit fasten upon people's minds that you are
other than you seem, sordid when you aim to be unselfish,
hypocritical when you seek to be devout, you can understand Mr. Bliss's feelings under such imputations.   Yet he
never gave visible token of it.

     "And he knew sore trials.   He knew what it was
to stand by the bedside of a beloved wife, and press
the hand that seems growing chill with the frost of death,
and be watching the face for the last look, and day
after day looking for the dreaded end to come.   It was
a marvel to me how he could go through this and be
so calm.   I thought it must be by a prodigious effort of
will; but I found, as I knew him better, that it was the con-
sciousness of God's tender presence and upbearing love
that sustained him.   His anchorage was ' within the vail,'
and he believed and proved that God would be as good as
His word, and keep him in perfect peace whose mind was
stayed upon Him.   So when the younger of these precious
children seemed daily slipping out of his embrace, and he
bent over the crib that he expected would so soon be empty,
to take what might prove the last kiss, his hopefulness
suffered no eclipse.   There seemed always to be an open
door between his soul and the city of light.

     "As might be anticipated, his hymns and music are full
of hope and exultation.   There is hardly a melancholy
verse or strain among them all.   Almost invariably both
songs and music swell and grow jubilant as they move on.
Hallelujahs ring all through them.   And not a few, however they begin, land us in the glory of the better country
before they close.   Glad tidings are indeed in them, and
are their inspiration.

     "When the sweet singer put his magnificent voice into the rendering, charged with the fervour of his sympathetic soul, as it was his delight to do, they that listened had a hint of what the joy of the Upper Presence will be. His buoyancy was contagious. I have known him, when a prayer-meeting dragged, when very likely the minister was dispirited and others shared the feeling, to sweep his hand over the keys of the piano, and alike by touch and voice scatter the despondency as a burst of sunshine scatters fog; and this because he sang as he felt. On one of the last occasions when he was with us, in a flying visit to our city made during his work as evangelist, he came in late and sat in the rear of the room. Espying him, I called him forward to sing the hymn entitled 'My Prayer.' He struck the piano keys, stopped, and reading the words in the latter part of the first stanza, 'More joy in His service,' said, ' I do not think I can sing that as a prayer any more. It seems to me I have as much joy in serving the blessed Master as it is possible for me to bear.'

"Then our brother was always glad to lend himself to every service whereby he could lighten the burdens of any afflicted heart. Now in the cottage of the day-labourer, now in the attics or tenement houses—where poverty and wretchedness abound; everywhere—he was to be found scattering gloom, upbearing faith, solacing aching hearts, preaching Christ with the marvels of his song. How often as he sang have the tears and sobs ceased, and the light broken in on the faces full of dismay! There are many homes where the music of that voice bringing God's comforts to the soul in its trouble, lingers in a memory that will never die.

" Naturally this unselfishness found its highest expression in devotion to the work of winning souls. Always single-hearted, and faithful in using his opportunities for doing good, after he took up evangelistic labour he came to have a

peculiar intensity of zeal in spiritual things.   He hungered
for more knowledge of Christ, more of the indwelling power
of the Spirit, and this to the end that he might save men.
In his later years, this desire was very marked.   His testimonies in social meetings always emphasized it; his daily
conversation had it for a constant theme; his appeals to
Sabbath-school children—his songs—were full of it.   Even
his ordinary correspondence, not only that of a friendly
character, but that relating to business, was permeated with
it.   From the letters I have seen, I am constrained to
believe that during the last three years, those letters, of
whatever kind, were exceptional, that did not contain some
word of earnest witness, encouragement, or appeal, in behalf
of Christ and His salvation.   I saw, the other day, a
purely business letter in which toward the end was a most
affectionate entreaty to accept Christ and live for Him.   I
remember a letter to a member of the choir, in which he
pressed upon her very earnestly the claims of her Saviour, and
she traces to that appeal the beginning of her life of faith.

And how many of you can bear like witness to his
solicitude for your salvation !   In how many of your homes
has he prayed during his transient home visits !   With how
many of you has he had personal interviews concerning your
eternal welfare !   How faithful he was to his Master and to
you in these last days of his fellowship on earth !   When he
instituted those Bible readings and pleaded for souls, neither
you nor he dreamed the end was so near, and that this was
his last work for the Lord he loved.   But if he had known
it, wherein could he have been more faithful ?   Up and
down this valley he went day after day, telling the ‘old, old
story,’ and seeking to persuade all who heard, to believe and
be saved : and, as I learn, nearly a score of new-born
souls rejoice to-day in the hope of eternal life through these
labours.

"This was his spirit always. He never had a choir rehearsal that was not opened with prayer; and the burden of his prayer was, that the singing might exalt Christ. In the centre of one of the stained windows of the transept of the church was a large crimson cross, and around it the words, 'God forbid that I should glory, save in the cross of our Lord Jesus Christ.' Mr. Bliss often called attention to that symbol and its motto, and said, 'I am glad the cross is always before us when we sing. Let us seek to forget ourselves and magnify Christ.'

"A little incident that occurred at the time of the burning of our church, in January, 1873, illustrates this. The front gable of the church was surmounted by a large cross, and underneath it was an immense window studded with purple stars. As the flames rolled up from within, the starry emblazonry shone out very beautifully; and when, climbing higher, they fairly garlanded the cross, and, standing there among the gleaming stars, it seemed to dash the fiery billows back as with majestic disdain, the sight was grandly impressive. Coming up to a young man, a member of the Sabbath school, Mr. Bliss laid his hand upon his shoulder, and said, 'James, why not give your heart to the Saviour to-night? Why not come to the cross this very hour? See it yonder! it was never so beautiful, never so dear to me as now.' And I have it from the lips of the young man, now a member of the church, that those words on the pavement brought him to a decision, and then and there he planted the cross in his heart. So this dear brother wrought ever. And no words could more truly set forth the one absorbing purpose that ruled his life, than those of one of his later and most effective pieces :—

> " 'My only song and story
>   Is—Jesus died for me ;
> My only hope of glory
>   The cross of Calvary.'

"Would that the thousands of Christian people whose hearts are saddened by this providence, might, through it, come to know a like spirit of coveting of souls !

"I name as a final characteristic that our brother was pre-eminently a singer of the Gospel. Taking both songs and music into the estimate, I think I may safely call him the Gospel singer of the age. Certainly I know of no one in the whole range of hymnology who has put Gospel truth into song with the clearness, and fulness, and power which stamps the compositions of P. P. Bliss. Many of his songs, especially his later ones, are little else than Scripture versified and set to music. Take, for example :—

> " ' Jesus of Nazareth passeth by,' *
> " ' Free from the Law,'
> " ' Look and Live,'
> " ' Whosoever Will may Come,'
> " ' Hear ye the Glad Good News from Heaven !'
> " ' Almost Persuaded,'
> " ' Seeking to Save,'
> " ' No other Name.'

"There is gospel enough in almost any one of them to lead a troubled soul to Christ. And in no hymns with which I am acquainted, not even Charles Wesley's, is the doctrine of salvation by the blood of Christ as the sacrifice for sin, so clearly stated, so fully emphasized ; and no wonder—these songs were born in the closet and at the foot of the cross.

"This is why, as Mr. Moody testifies, no songs so lay hold of the people's heart. In words and music they are surcharged with the very spirit of the gospel. And herein lies

---

* This does not refer to the better-known hymn of Miss Campbell on this passage.

the secret of the power which they are destined to wield in after years. Take the Hymns that have wrought themselves imperishably into the affections of God's people, such, for example, as —

> " ' Rock of Ages,'
> " ' Just as I am,'
> " ' Nearer, my God, to Thee,'
> " ' Jesus, Lover of My Soul,'
> " ' All hail the Power of Jesus' Name ; '

and what is the reason of the place they hold? Obviously this, that they embody truths which go to the heart of the gospel, truths that have to do with the most vital experiences of the soul in seeking and working out salvation. So of these songs of Philip Bliss. And this is why the Chinese and the Zulus sing them. They do not sing 'Hail, Columbia,' or the 'Star-spangled Banner.' They do not care for the story of our native land; they have no interest in either its past or its future. But the story of Jesus Christ, of the Lamb slain that sinners might have pardon, that story finds a response in their hearts. They know they are in darkness. They know they are in trouble. They know the curse of sin binds its yokes upon their souls, keeps its cry of woe upon their lips. And when they hear these songs, they recognize the offer of help, the opening-up of a way of deliverance. In a word, the conscious want of men the world over is—Christ; and these songs preach Him. They preach Him so fully, that if a ship were wrecked in some archipelago, where no missionary has ever yet set foot, and the survivors should have no Bliss, nothing but a copy of the 'Gospel Songs,' I should expect in five years to find churches and Sunday schools and revivals and missions among the heathen round about.

"They have been most wonderfully blessed already. At

the farewell meeting in London, after the labours of Brother Moody and Brother Sankey were closed in that city, Lord Shaftesbury said that ' if Mr. Sankey had done no more than teach the people to sing " Hold the Fort," he would have conferred an inestimable blessing on the British Empire.' Mr. Sankey bears witness that these songs laid hold of the English people with wonderful power. Major Cole says, ' the ragged children of London, children who are largely street waifs, living in the utmost ignorance and degradation, flocked to hear and sing these songs till they had ten thousand of them at a gathering.' And to this day, they are to be heard in the streets, in the courtyards, stables, shops, factories, homes, everywhere. Alike among the rich and the poor, mothers rock their babes to sleep with them. Nobility and peasantry find common inspiration in them, and to the suffering and dying of every rank they minister inexpressible blessing.

" But their grandest work, at home and abroad, has been in preaching the gospel and winning souls. Let me give a single illustration of many connected with the recent revival services in Chicago. One of the reformed inebriates says that he had been for years one of the hardest of drinkers. His friends had given him up as a hopeless case, and he had given up himself and expected to die as he lived, and meet a drunkard's awful doom. In this condition he came to Chicago ; and one day, when more than half-intoxicated, he wandered aimlessly with the crowd into the Tabernacle, and found a seat in the gallery. He was too intoxicated to know much about what was going on, and did not remember anything about the text or the sermon. During the evening, Mr. Sankey sang ' What shall the Harvest be ? ' And when he came to the words,

> " ' Sowing the seed of a lingering pain,
> Sowing the seed of a maddened brain,

Sowing the seed of a tarnished name,
Sowing the seed of eternal shame ;
Oh, what shall the harvest be ? '

the singer's voice rang through the inebriate like the trump
of the Judgment, and fairly sobered him. Conscience, so
long dead, was suddenly roused, and began to lash him with
the words of the song. His wasted, wretched life passed
in painful review before him. The promise of his youth
blighted ; the ambitions and hopes of manhood turned to
ashes ; his family beggared and disgraced ; his name a by-
word of shame ; his friends among the pure and good all
alienated, and his fellowship only with the low and vile ; his
whole career one dark, damning record of folly and sin ; and
before him a gathering night of hopeless despair—he could not
endure the torment of such a vision. It was hell before the
time. So he went out, and tried to drown the song in drink.
But it would not die. It rang in his ears by day and by
night, and forced him again and again to the Tabernacle.
By and by his sin so burdened him that he went to Mr.
Sawyer's inquiry room ; and there God met him, took his
feet out of the horrible pit, planted them on the Rock, and
put a new song into his mouth. And now he is seeking,
with all his might, to help others, who are bound by the same
curse, to find the blessed liberty of the Gospel.

"This is only one case of scores, that during this single
revival have been led into the Kingdom through the agency
of these Hymns. So it has been elsewhere ; so it will continue to be. I believe, with Mr. Moody, that God raised
up Philip Bliss, as truly as He did Charles Wesley to save
men by singing the Gospel. And herein lies the guarantee of
a mighty harvest of souls in the days to come. Few of us
have ever read John Wesley's or Isaac Barrow's sermons ;
but there are none of us who do not sing Charles Wesley's
hymns, and Isaac Watts's versions of the Psalms. Rela-

tively to the singer's, the preacher's horizon is an exceedingly
narrow one. He may reach the men of his city, his country,
his age, possibly a handful in other lands and in after-years ;
but the singer's voice ranges all lands, all ages. Not only
does it not die, but it gathers potency with every cycle of
years. Such hymns as 'Rock of Ages,' 'Just as I Am,'
' My Faith looks up to Thee,' will be sung as long as there
are saints to be helped or sinners to be saved. Every generation will only widen their influence and magnify their
power as agencies which God delights to honour. I do not
hesitate to say that some of my Brother Bliss's songs will go
down the future side by side with these in their ministry of
Christ and salvation. And the fruitage of his life before
God called him, blessed as it was—compared with that which
shall yet be garnered—will prove only as the firstfruits to an
ingathering which only the arithmetic of heaven can measure.
He dropped the seed by handfuls, but the harvest shall
wave like Lebanon.

  " While I say these things, I do not forget how thoroughly
identified with our brother in all his aims and work, was his
dear wife, over whose early going home we both mourn and
rejoice to-day. She not only cheerfully accepted the call of
Providence which took her husband so largely from home,
but with constant and potent aid of voice and pen she
helped to crown his work with abundant success. He
appreciated such co-operation, and often recognized it,
saying that he ' was more indebted to his wife than any one
else for what he was and what he had done.' ' Lovely and
pleasant in their lives, in their death they were not divided.'
Their memories are alike precious, and their works will
alike follow them.

  " In the mountains of the Tyrol, it is the custom of the
mothers, and wives, and children, to go forth when the
twilight gathers, to welcome home their husbands, fathers,

and sons, from their care of the flocks up the mountain heights ; and as they go they sing a strain or two of some national air, and then listen, till apparently from the clouds there float down to them the answering refrains, and they know that all is well, and that ere long they will see the faces and be clasped in the arms of those they love. Something like this may we not venture to imagine here ? In the deepening twilight of our sorrow we lift our eyes to the uplands of the better country, longing for the fellowship of these dear departed ones. And as we look, the sweet strains they taught us, and which we were wont to sing together, break instinctively from our lips ; and lo, in the pauses of our song there seems to float down to us from the heavenly heights the refrain borrowed from our lips, ' Watching and waiting for you.' Dear friends, we are the pilgrims, and these who have gone before are the ones ' at home ;' and a little way on, a few more steps only of this rough and thorny way—after a few more pains, and griefs, and tears, and a little more blessed toil for Christ and for souls—we shall receive their welcome, share their joy, and abide in our Father's house for ever."

At the close of Dr. Goodwin's address, Major Whittle announced as a closing song a hymn that had just been found among Mr. Bliss's papers—the music and chorus of which were probably among his latest compositions—entitled " He knows." The hymn, which was at first believed to have been written by Mr. Bliss, was really from the pen of Miss M. G. Brainerd, and will be found in full on page 113.

> " So on I go, not knowing ;
>   I would not if I might :
> I'd rather walk in the dark with God,
>   Than go alone in the light ;
> I'd rather walk by faith with Him,
>   Than go alone by sight."

Memorial Services were also held at Chicago. The
tidings of the catastrophe had fallen on the heart of that
great city with a suddenness that at first forbad belief. On
the following Sabbath Mr. Moody's Tabernacle was draped
in mourning from the platform to the galleries; and near
the speaker were four white crowns of camellias and pure
white lilies, for at that time it was supposed that the whole
family had gone up to heaven. The immense multitude in
that crowded church looked through their tears on Mr.
Moody as he entered, broken down under that weight of
affliction. With a terrible struggle to keep back the sobs
and tears, he rose and repeated the words, " Know ye not
that there is a prince and a great man fallen in Israel!"
He could add no more than a request for silent prayer.
Amidst the subdued signs of overpowering emotion, the
Rev. Dr. Chamberlain was heard giving thanks to Christ for
the hope of eternal life. At length the congregation were
able to join in singing—

> " ' In the Christian's home in glory
> There remains a land of rest.' "

The Rev. Dr. Thompson afterwards spoke, and told how
he was singing the hymns of Mr. Bliss by the sick beds of
weary sufferers in another State, when the telegram came of
the translation of the author. " He has now learned," said
the speaker, " the meaning of his own words—

> " ' The form of the mansion fair,
> And the song that the angels sing."

and he added, " Once when I was speaking to our now
glorified brother, he said, with a smile : ' I sing for Christ :
I have not even a home to my name.' "

The Rev. Dr. Williamson now led the congregation in
prayer on behalf of the heavily-afflicted relatives, and espe-

cially of the parents whose children had gone to their corona-
tion. Mr. Moody, after he had spoken of his love to their
" sweet singer," suggested with his usual practical ability the
appointment of two committees and a treasurer, who should
be charged with the task of erecting a suitable monument
to the memory of the dead, and a collection was at once
made, " the only one ever taken in the Tabernacle."*

In the after-part of the Sabbath, Mr. Sankey was able
to sing Mr. Bliss's " Watching and Waiting," and his
" When Jesus comes," which created a profound impression
on the audience. Mr. Moody, better able to speak than in
the morning, addressed the congregation from the words,
" Be ye also ready." At times, however, his words were
unintelligible, for he spoke with difficulty. He warned of
death, and urged the necessity of regeneration and repentance. The verse was sung—

> " I gave My life for thee,
>   My precious blood I shed
> That thou might'st ransomed be,
>   And quickened from the dead—
> I gave, I gave My life for thee ;
>   What hast thou given for Me ? "

Mr. Moody prayed long and earnestly for the unsaved
souls, and invoked the richest outpourings of mercy on the
obstinate hearts. At times during the prayer he stopped for
some minutes, utterly unable to control his emotions.

On the following Friday, January 5th, 1877, it is said
that at least 12,000 people were gathered within and with-

---

* Happily the parents, quite contrary to what their friends had
understood of their intention, had left in Pennsylvania, with their
relatives, their two little boys, Paul, four years, and George, two years
old. A fund has generously been founded in the United States for their
benefit.

out the Tabernacle. The service was expository and musical.
They sang the hymn of Mr. Bliss—

> " Hallelujah ! 'tis done, I believe on the Son,
>   I am saved by the blood of the Crucified One ;"

also " Beneath the Cross of Jesus," " Will you meet me at
the Fountain ? " " Only an Armour-Bearer," " Fading away
like the Stars of the Morning," " Weary Gleaner, whence
comest Thou ? " " Whosoever Will ;" and the children sang
with great sweetness, " I am so glad that Jesus loves me."
The whole congregation sang " Hold the Fort." It was
stated on the occasion that " Professor Bliss was seen by a
passenger whose life was spared, sitting in a car by the side
of his wife, with his open Bible on his knee, and both
seemed intently engaged in the study of the Sacred Word,
while he was composing a Bible song which earth was never
to hear ; and this is the last we know of them in the body."

Chapter XIII.

EMORIAL SERVICES were held at the Reformed Church, South Bend, Indiana; at St. Paul, Minnesota; at Louisville, Kentucky; at Nashville, Tennessee; at Kalamazoo, Michigan; at Peoria, Illinois, and other places. Thus widespread was the mourning; and the catholic spirit of the man they mourned was evidenced in the union of all Christian congregations with their pastors.

Tributes also were offered to his memory by editors, clergymen, and musical writers, in all parts of America. Some of these are quoted to show the unanimity of opinion respecting him. The editor of the *Inter-Ocean* says :—

"Mr. Bliss was a fine specimen of a vigorous and robust man. He was gifted with a sweet voice and an attractive manner. He carried into his musical work the martial bearing and movement of the commander in a great crusade. This spirit breathes along his lines, and swells in all his music. Children quickly caught this heroic spirit. His military figures found the nation responsive. He is never, in any composition, at a halt. He is always marching forward or struggling upward. There is always the suggestion of the leader's plume to the front; there is always a purpose, a hope, a promise, a resolve, at the heart; there is always present the spirit that moves masses to responsive or heroic moods, or that pathos which calls out the best there is in man. Hence the popularity of Mr. Bliss's compositions, and, more important, the good influence they have exerted."

Harper's Weekly speaks in similar terms, and of Mr. Bliss's special work in popularizing the religious movement of the day, which has so visibly affected the masses of the population in England, Scotland, Ireland, and America.

The *Advance*, with like discrimination, says in an article by Simeon Gilbert :—

"No doubt some of Mr. Bliss's hymns will, having met a special want in the development of the Christian life of the period, and served their temporary, but not on that account unimportant, use, pass away; but some of them, we are confident, will take their place among those which the church will not let die. Those who shall hereafter pause to trace the distinctive qualities, the *timbre*, so to speak, of the Christian life of this time, will note that what Charles Wesley was to John Wesley, Mr. Bliss has been to Mr. Moody.

"The best of Mr. Bliss's hymns and tunes are simple and lucid utterances of the heart of the Gospel, and of the Christian experience of those who put complete trust in Christ as a perfect Saviour. Not keyed to the same pitch as Luther's famous battle hymn, 'A strong tower is our God,' he yet gauged the popular temper and want of the churches equally well. The present more particularly aggressive form of evangelistic work owes as much to what Mr. Bliss and his singing co-labourers have contributed as to any other human instrumentality.

"In George Herbert's 'Country Parson,' the parson

preaching is told that he must first ' dip in his own heart ' his words before he speaks them. Mr. Bliss had experienced his own songs before he composed them. It is not claimed that he was a great poet, or that he possessed the genius for some of the sublimer strains of music, but he had the sense and the tact which are not often equalled in matching words and tunes, and suiting both to the popular requirement."

Mr. Philip Phillips writes in similar terms of Mr. Bliss's " rare gifts." Mr. G. C. Needham, the eminent evangelist, speaks of his " princely manners," and of his " rare worth, grace, and spiritual attainments." The Rev. J. B. Atchinson, of Detroit, says, " There is no uninspired man, living or dead, who exerted such a powerful influence over me as he did."

The Rev. Dr. J. H. Brookes, of St. Louis, writes that the last night of 1876, unto the midnight hour, was spent by his people in tears, and continual prayers, and meditations on the Word, after the terrible tidings had fallen on the city. " The elders," he says, " came to my study and told me with sobs that Bliss had been killed. Oh, in the presence of such a sore affliction, how our hearts cry out, ' Even so, come, Lord Jesus.' How pitifully little the world seems ! how contemptible self ! how near eternity !"

Rev. George T. Ladd, of Milwaukee, speaks of " the joy " it was to work with Mr. Bliss, and states that the converts of his services a year ago stand well.

Dr. Baird, Presbyterian pastor at Nashville, testifies to the striking simplicity of Mr. Bliss's character, and his Christian devotedness to the cause of Christ, and how precious his memory was.

These testimonies might be largely multiplied. They are adduced to show that it was not upon one, but upon all sections of the Church of Christ, that the catholic spirit of Mr. Bliss had produced a profound impression. From all classes also have come evidences of the usefulness of his hymns. "Eternity alone," writes one, "can reveal to us the part Mr. Bliss's songs have had in the rescue of our fallen humanity." In Boston a man who was giving the clearest evidence of a change of heart stood up and testified that all his views of the "Word of life" were changed by hearing Sunday-school children singing, "Jesus loves me." In Scotland constant testimonies to the value of this hymn were given in the inquiry-room to Mr. Moody.

A missionary of the American Sunday-school Union in Missouri, after he had organized a Sunday-school recently, sang to them—

"I am so glad that Jesus loves me,"

and followed it with the question, "Are you glad? If not, why?" He had hardly finished when a young man rose, and rushing up to him, sobbed out, "Oh, sir, you must not leave here until I am a Christian!" Prayer was offered for him, and he cast his soul on Christ. Then he exclaimed, "Oh, that song! I could not get away from it; and it has saved me."

In England, a young woman ignorant of the Gospel went into a Meeting, and said afterwards that while this same hymn was being sung, for the first time in her life she saw that she was a sinner. All her sins came up in array before her; she said in her heart, "Jesus cannot love me; He could not love such a sinner as I am." She went home in a state of extreme mental anguish, and did not sleep that night. Every opportunity of obtaining more light was eagerly seized. She took her place in the "inquiry-room." There she found, to her astonishment and joy, that Jesus *could*, DID, DOES love sinners. She saw in God's opened Word that it was for sinners Jesus died, and for none others.

Of the same hymn, another Christian worker records :—
" One day a lady called on me when I first held classes for children, and said, 'There is a little singing girl belonging to one of your classes who is dying. She wants you to go and see her.' I went to her home, a little frame cottage ; and there I found a little maid dying, one whom I had known so well in the Thursday evening meetings. I said, ' My dear child, how is it with you ? ' ' Will you pray for my father and mother as you pray for us ? ' she enquired. ' But how is it with yourself ? ' I again asked. ' Oh, sir,' she answered, 'they tell me I am about to die, but I have found the Lord Jesus Christ.' ' When did you become a Christian ? ' I inquired. ' Don't you remember one Thursday when you were teaching me to sing—

> " I am so glad that Jesus loves me,
> Jesus loves me, Jesus loves me ; "

and don't you remember you told us that if we only gave our hearts to Him, He would love us ?—and I gave mine to Him.'
" What that little dying girl said to me helped to cheer me on more than anything I had heard before, because she was my first convert. Thank God, there have been many since."

In Philadelphia an attorney joined the church under the care of Dr. Reed, and confessed that the means of his decision was Mr. Bliss's " Almost Persuaded." This happily is one, out of many cases, where God has given His blessing to that pleading hymn.

Rev. H. Burton, of Bradford, England, writes that he once wrote to convey to Mr. Bliss the obligations of many, for his hymns and music. He replied as follows :—

" Thanks for your complimentary mention of the songs I have had the pleasure of writing. You need not call them mine. If there is any good in any of them, it came from Him, the Source of all. To Him be all the praise."

The following is taken from a publication called the " Youth's Companion : "—

" On the stage at one of the Liverpool theatres, a comic singer came out before the footlights to sing. Just as he was about to commence his waggish melody, the tune of a sweet Sunday-school hymn, learned before, came suddenly to mind, and so confused him that he completely forgot his part. He stood a moment trying to recall it, and then retired, covered with shame. The manager, enraged at his failure, and still more enraged at his apparently foolish explanation, paid him the remainder of his wages, and ordered him at once to quit his service. Out of employment, he wandered about the city like the unclean spirit, seeking rest and finding none. His heart was full of curses, and to drown his mortification he drank deep and desperately, till his days and nights were one continual debauch.

" In the meantime, Mr. Moody and Mr. Sankey began their Meetings in Liverpool. The fame of the Evangelists was in every mouth, and the young actor, hearing them discussed and ridiculed among his low associates, conceived the idea of writing a burlesque about them to be put upon the stage. He sobered himself sufficiently to begin. But he felt he could not make his work complete without more ' points ' or ' hits ' to give it zest. So he determined to attend a meeting himself, and hear the men whom he

intended to lampoon. He went, and the same power that
in the sudden memory of that early hymn had driven him
once from the stage arrested him and held him a reverent
listener. At the close he remained among the penitent
inquirers, and was soon led to accept the Lord Jesus as his
Master. The young man is now preparing himself for
Christian work.

"That simple Sunday-school song, to the poor comedian,
was a voice come back from his by-gone and better days.
In spite of himself it changed his fate, and led the way to
the still better days beyond."

The Rev. J. N. Carman, Baptist pastor, of Indianapolis,
writes what can scarcely surprise us :—"An aged and scep-
tical gentleman in Norwalk, Ohio, dated his convictions,
which led him to Christ, to hearing Mrs. Carman sing Mr.
Bliss's 'If Papa were only Ready.'"

Letters from all parts of the world keep coming in
which bear the same testimony of blessing given to the
words of the departed one. But we have only room for
one written from Chicago on March 8th, 1877 :—

"In response to your request, I communicate the following facts in regard to my life, and conversion through
the instrumentality of that song by Mr. Bliss, 'What shall
the Harvest Be?'

"At the breaking out of the war, in 1861, I hastened to
take service in the army, and soon after—in August of that
year—I was appointed a First Lieutenant in the regular
army. At that time, I was not yet eighteen years of age,
and never had been away from home influences. I had
never tasted any kind of intoxicating liquor, and did not
know one card from another. The regiment to which I
was assigned was principally officered by young men, many
of whom were old in dissipation. The new life was an

attractive one, and I entered upon it with avidity. In a very few months I became a steady drinker and a constant card player. I do not remember to have made any attempt to resist the encroachments of vice ; on the contrary, I took a mad delight in all forms of dissipation. I laughed at the caution of older heads, and asserted, with all the egotism of a boy, that I could abandon my bad habits at any time. But the time speedily came when I recognized the fact that my evil desires had obtained the complete mastery of my will, and that I was no longer able to exercise any control over myself. From that hour I knew no peace. The years that followed were but a succession of struggles against the dominion of my appetite, and a repetition of failures. With each failure, I lost something of my power of resistance and gained something of evil. In 1870 I resigned my commission and returned to civil life, determined to make one last stand against my passions by breaking away from my old associations and beginning a new life. The result was attained in my condition a few months ago. I do not like to recall the past six years. They are as a frightful dream, from which, thank God ! I was at last awakened ; but the recollection of which will always bring sorrow and remorse.

" When the Tabernacle was opened last fall, I was in Chicago, presumably on my way to Minnesota. Only a few weeks before I had left my family, promising with my last words that I would stop drinking, and try once more to be a sober man. I did not keep the promise five minutes ; I *could* not. I stopped here, actuated by a desire to indulge, unrestrained, my appetite for liquor and cards, and in those few weeks I had taken a fearful plunge downward. At last I made up my mind that there was absolutely no hope for me, and I wanted the end to come quickly. I gave myself up to the wildest debauchery, and speculated with a reckless indifference on how much longer my body could endure

the fearful strain.   In anticipation of sudden death, I carefully destroyed all evidences of my identity, so that my
friends might never know the dog's death I had died.   It
was while in this condition that I one day wandered into
the Tabernacle, and found a seat in the gallery.   I looked
at the happy faces about me, and I hated them.   I had all
the vindictive feeling of a wild animal hunted to his last
covert, and waiting in impotent rage the final blow that is
to end his miserable life.   I did not pay much attention to
the service.   I was drowsy and stupefied with liquor.   But
after awhile there was a perfect stillness, out of which presently rose the voice of Mr. Sankey (may God for ever
bless him!) in Mr. Bliss's song, 'What shall the harvest
be?' The words and music attracted my attention, and
I was aroused to listen.   They stirred me with a strange
sensation; and when presently he sang —

> " ' Sowing the seed of a lingering pain,
> Sowing the seed of a maddened brain,
> Sowing the seed of a tarnished name,
> Sowing the seed of eternal shame,
> Oh, what shall the harvest be?'

the words pierced me like an arrow.   My deadened conscience was aroused, and with one swift glance memory
recalled my bright boyhood, my wasted manhood, and
showed me my lost opportunities.   Every word of the song
was true of my own case, and in bitter agony I was reaping
the harvest my misdeeds had brought me.   I thought of
my old mother, of my loving, faithful wife and children, and
of how they, too, were compelled to reap of my harvest of
dishonour.   My awakened conscience lashed me as with a
whip of scorpions, and I rushed from the Tabernacle, and
sought to drown its voice in more whiskey.   But it was of
no use.   Wherever I went, whether to the bar of the saloon,
or to the gaming table, or to the solitude of my own room,

before my eyes in letters of fire were always the words,
'What shall the harvest be?'

"For two weeks I endured this torture, having no rest,
until at last on my knees I cried to God for mercy, and He
heard my prayer. Broken, weak, vile, and helpless, I came
to Him, believing that 'the blood of Jesus Christ His Son
cleanseth us from *all* sin,' and trusting that His love and
compassion would regard even me. And, Major, I have
not trusted in vain. He has removed from me my old
desires and appetites, and made me a new creature in
Christ Jesus. He has guided me, shielded me, and fought
my battles for me ; and day by day my faith grows brighter,
and my love stronger.

"'The Lord is my rock, and my fortress, and my de-
liverer ; my God, my strength, in whom I will trust ; my
buckler, and the horn of my salvation, and my high tower.'

"Very truly, your friend and brother in Christ,

"W. O. L."

Let it not, however, be thought that the usefulness of
Mr. Bliss is over. It may be that the Lord will give to his
hymns a more extended blessing when there is associated
with them the knowledge of his entire consecration and of his
full-orbed character. How might the ladies of England in
hundreds of parishes attract the loiterers of the village, shed
gladness over the "monotonous and colourless" lives of
English labourers, and bring them to the knowledge of
salvation in Christ, by erecting or engaging a plain room,
and, with the accompaniment of piano or harmonium,
singing to them these Gospel hymns of Mr. Bliss, and
telling them about the self-less life of him who was once
"a country boy!" Often, when there is no evening service
in the hamlet, men and youths stand on a Sunday night in
groups, unwilling to go to the ale-house, and would be glad

to be welcomed to such a meeting. This is not asking ladies to preach, but to consecrate to God, and to those who have few bright hours in life, the talents which they use to make their own drawing-rooms pleasant.

In the book called "LATER SONGS AND SOLOS" there are nineteen hymns of Mr. Bliss's, which are little known among us, besides his thrilling music to such words as, "Oh, the Clanging Bells of Time," and "Lift up thy Voice," and "Oppressed by the Noonday's Scorching Heat," etc. Religious feeling and the sympathetic sentiment of poetic culture are indispensable in singing these later productions of his pen. The harmonies are more complex and the bass more varied and expressive than in his earlier sacred songs. They should be sung with the inspiration of a heart sanctified by prayer. To sing them as an amusement is to destroy their value, and subvert their purpose. Exquisitely sweet and touching among these his later hymns, are such as "At the feet of Jesus;" "How Much Owest Thou?" "In Me ye may have Peace;" "In Zion's Rock Abiding;" "Tenderly the Shepherd;" "See the gentle Shepherd Standing," and "Man of Sorrows," etc. How suited would these be for the voices of a few Christian ladies in such services as have been above indicated!

It is the fashion in some quarters to affect an indifference to all such hymns, and to utter depreciatory words about them. It must, however, be remembered that, while in matters of intellectual acquisition the five out of a thousand may be right and the rest wholly wrong: in matters of the deepest human emotions, the five may be wholly incompetent to touch and move the heart of the bulk of mankind. If they are wise men, they will not disparage this *highest result* of music by whomsoever it may be produced. Can we have any better standard of the value of music than the effect it produces? May not another standard be altogether

artificial and arbitrary? To complain that Mr. Bliss's songs
and music are not to be compared with other productions,
is to do him great injustice. He never intended a com-
parison. But he wished to teach God our Father's love to
us in Jesus in words and strains that would go direct to the
heart; and the Lord helped him to do this.

Of himself he would have said, as did the prophet Amos
of Tekoa, " I was no prophet, neither was I a prophet's son ;
but I was a herdman, and a gatherer of sycamore fruit ; and
the Lord took me as I followed the flock, and the Lord said
unto me, ' Go, prophesy unto my people Israel.' " (Amos
vii. 14, 15.)

Reduced Fac-simile Copy of Letter (with some few omissions) written by Mr. P. P. Bliss to the Publishers, a short time before his death.

Chicago, Oct 9. 1876

Messrs Morgan & Scott
      London, Eng.

    Gentlemen :-

      Your ....
....
.... is this day received

    Please to accept my most
heartfelt thanks, dear Sirs, for
the grace thus freely bestowed

    Five years ago this day was
the great "Chicago Fire" in which
my business "went up", as we say

    I must acknowledge, however,
that since that time, I have been
enjoying greater prosperity in the
best sense of the word, than ever
before. For much of it I owe under
God, a debt of gratitude to you.

I am glad to hear from Messrs. Moody & Sankey that .... one of your house may come over .... I shall be happy in a personal acquaintance. The meetings here are grand and glorious; though, as you may have heard, Bro. Moody is, for a few days, called to Northfield, by the death suddenly, of his youngest brother; who — praise the Lord — was converted about a year ago

With high respect and many, many thanks

I am musically and truly yours

P. P. Bliss

My Grandfather's Bible.

A CENTENNIAL SONG.

1. The Sabbath day—sweet day of rest— Was draw-ing to a close; The
2. "Old friend," said I, "if thou couldst tell, What would thy mem'ries be?" And

summer breeze went mur-m'ring by, To lull me to re - pose: I
from the Book there seemed to come This ev' -ning rev - er - ie: "Good

took my fa - ther's bi - ble down— His fa - ther's gift to him— A
will to men, Peace be to thee! My mis - sion aye hath been,

trea-sure rare, be-yond compare, Though soiled the page, and dim.

2nd time omit.

To tell the love of Him who died To save a world from sin.

3. A hundred years a-go I sailed, With those who sail no more, Through

per-ils dread by land and sea, I reached New Eng-land's shore; There,

on a soul-worn, faithful band This sooth - ing psalm did ·fall:

Lord, Thou hast been our dwell-ing place, In gen - e - ra - tions all.

Year after year, in temples rude, Up - on the desk I lay, To

teach of Him, the Great High Priest; The Life, the Truth, the Way.

And multitudes who listened there To God's life - giv - ing word,

Are rest - ing from their la-bours now, "For e - ver with the Lord."

Anon a lowly home I found, But Love and Peace were there, .. The

children with the father read, And knelt with him in prayer;

And through the valley, as one passed, I heard her sweet - ly sing :—

"O Grave, where is thy vic - to - ry? O Death, where is thy sting?"

"Hold fast the faith," the old Book said, "Thy fa - ther's God a - dore; . .

And on the 'Rock of Ages' rest Thy soul for ev - er - more."

"A-men," said I, "by grace I will, Till at His feet we fal', And join the ev-er-last-ing song, And crown Him Lord of All. We'll join the ev-er-last-ing song, And crown Him Lord . . of All.

My Redeemer.

The last piece written by Mr. P. P. Bliss. (See page 79.)

P. P. BLISS.   JAMES McGRANAHAN.

1. I will sing of my Re-deem-er And His won-drous love to me;
2. I will tell the wondrous sto-ry, How my lost es-tate to save,
3. I will praise my dear Re-deem-er, His tri-umph-ant power I'll tell,
4. I will sing of my Re-deem-er And His heaven-ly love to me;

On the cru - el cross He suf - fered, From the curse to set me free.
In His bound-less love and mer - cy, He the ran - som free - ly gave.
How the vic - to - ry He giv - eth O - ver sin, and death and hell.
He from death to life hath brought me, Son of God, with Him to be.

CHORUS.

Sing, oh sing, ... of my Re - deem - er, With His
Sing, oh sing of my Redeemer, Sing, oh sing of my Redeem-er, With His

blood . . . . He pur-chased me, ... On the
blood He pur-chased me, With His blood He pur-chased me; On the

cross . . . He sealed my par - - don, Paid the

Repeat pp after last verse.

debt, and made me free, And made me free, and made me free.

When My Weary Hands are Folded.

"When thou passest through the waters."—Isa. xliii. 2.

P. P. Bliss.

Ira D. Sankey.

1. When my wea-ry hands are fold-ed on my faint-ly throbbing breast,
And my soul has spread her pin-ions for the ci-ty of the blest;
'Twill be sweet to hear the loved ones sing some dear fa-mil-iar song,
As I rise to join the cho-rus of the blood-washed, ho-ly throng.

2. But a greater joy 'twill give me if some toiling one can say,
I have helped to bear his burden and have cheered him on the way;
Oh! I'll praise His grace for ever who hath died to ransom me,
And hath chosen me a sharer in His blessed work to be.

3. When the songs of earth are over, and my last "good bye" is said,
When my lifeless form they follow to the dwelling of the dead:
'Twill be sweet if friends remember and shall mark the quiet spot,
Telling only that the sleeper hath not quickly been forgot.

4. But if one poor weary wanderer shall be guided home by me,
'Twere a grander, nobler monument throughout all eternity;
And to Him shall be the glory, unto whom all praise is due,
For the love that hath redeemed us, and hath made my heaven *two*.

5 When among the ransomed millions by His grace redeemed I stand,
Then my song shall swell the chorus of the glad triumphant band;
Oh, how sweet will be the resting when my conflicts all are past!
Oh, the mighty "Alleluia" of our victory at last!